CONTENTS

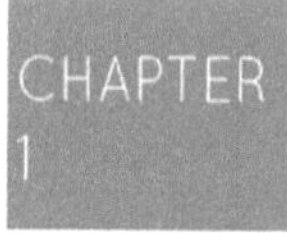

Americans and Their Pets

If you're like me, you watch those "save the animals" commercials with a lump in your throat. As soulful music plays in the background, you watch photo after photo of homeless animals with big eyes and pleading expressions, many of them locked behind a chain link fence or wandering in horrible circumstances. After seeing these pitiful creatures, we are moved to send a check for a few dollars or we promise to send a monthly contribution.

The need is great—not only in America, but also in other countries where the idea of helping homeless animals hasn't even made it onto the national priority list. I have visited countries in South America, for instance, where skinny dogs, many of them obvious new mothers, roam the streets, wary and frightened, searching for a bite of food. No one worries about their happiness; no one takes the time to photograph them for a televised plea.

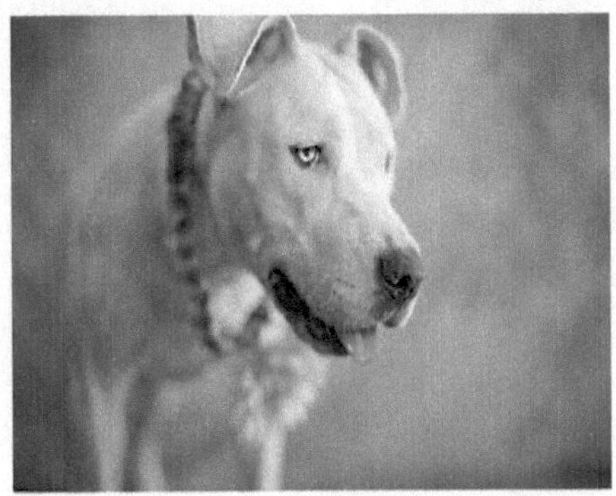

I recently became aware of a situation in Taiwan that breaks my heart. Tou Chih-kang, a Taiwanese photographer, takes photos of shelter dogs, too—but he takes photos of the dogs just before they are euthanized. The Taiwanese government euthanizes 80,000 dogs each year, most of them strays taken off the streets. In publishing his photos, Tou Chih-kang is hoping that people will wake up to the destruction of life going on all around them. You can read more of the story at: http://news.yahoo.com/photos/photographer-s-crusade-to-save-doomed-shelter-dogs-slideshow/ .

Not everyone ignores the plight of stray animals. I'm happy to report that a team of vets from my local animal hospital travels to South America every year to neuter and spay homeless dogs and cats. I'm sure veterinarians from other communities undertake similar ventures.

According to the SPCA, we can't begin to estimate how many homeless cats and dogs roam free in the United States—the number of cats alone may be as high as seventy million. One single fertile cat may have two litters per year, with four to six kittens in each litter. A fertile dog may have one litter a year, with an average of four to six puppies. These kittens and puppies will be able to reproduce within a year, and so the problem grows exponentially.

The answer to domestic animal overpopulation is spaying or neutering, but only 10 percent of the animals taken in at shelters have been spayed or neutered. Yet the cost of spaying or neutering a pet is less than the cost of raising puppies or kittens for a year.

Most people—including me—shudder when we hear about "kill shelters" where animals are euthanized, but few shelters have enough room or food or supplies or volunteers to deal with so many domestic animals, many of which suffer from severe medical or behavioral problems. Few shelters have the financial means to adopt a "no euthanasia" policy without turning other animals away.

At the shelter where I volunteer, I have been deeply impressed by the variety of committed people who come in every week to walk the dogs, train the dogs, care for the cats, photograph the animals, socialize and, if need be, foster pets with special needs. While the kennel environment can be stressful for some animals, I've been impressed at how often volunteers take time to spend time with these cats, dogs, birds, bunnies, horses, goats, and ponies.

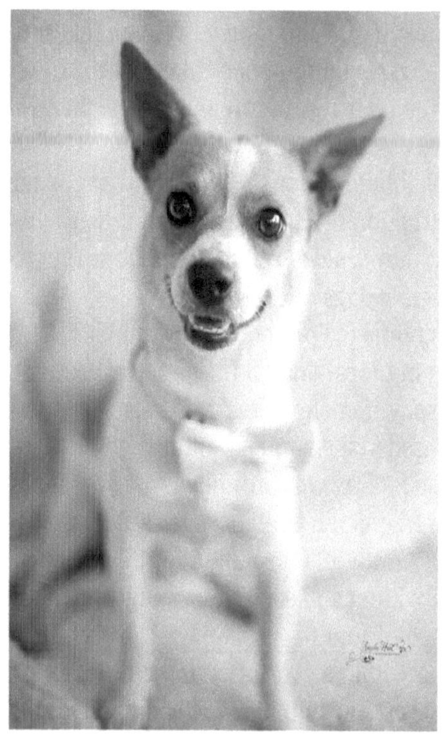

Our nation is producing more than enough domestic animals—we have no shortage of puppies, kittens, bunnies, or even reptiles. Puppy mills breed dogs like factories and sell to pet stores; "backyard breeders" produce puppies and advertise in the paper, often without checking the pedigree or health of the sire and dam. Worse still, owners who do not spay their female dogs and cats may find themselves with a "surprise pregnancy" and no idea what sort of pups they will be producing in a few short weeks. Animals from all of these categories find their way into shelters—purebreds and "accidents" alike.

People surrender their pets for all kinds of reasons, ranging from changes in family circumstances to a lack of time to properly train and exercise a dog. In a poor economy, more than a few families have to give up their pets for financial reasons—they simply can't afford to feed and provide medical care for their companion animals.

Though I am sorry to see this happen, I am glad they are choosing to make a responsible decision and bring their animals to a shelter or rescue group. Unfortunately, too many people simply take their pets to a neighborhood or field and turn them loose, assuming that someone else will pick them up and take care of them. That is simply being irresponsible. Not only are they abandoning their lost and bewildered pet, but the animal is at risk of being struck by a car, becoming involved in a fight with another animal, being overtaken by parasites, or starving.

Speaking of parasites, did you know that a single flea can bite its host 400 times a day? So if a dog has only ten fleas, it is suffering 4,000 bites every twenty-four hours. Heavy flea infestations can kill an animal, especially if it is sick or young. Dogs are also at risk of attracting ticks, heart worms, and other parasites.

Few animals are completely hopeless, and I believe all pets deserve a chance to find a new home. Unfortunately, many pets arrive at shelters sick or so emotionally damaged that only long-term behavior training could improve an animal's temperament . . . and few shelters have the time or the volunteers to undertake such training.

I have seen impressive shelters and rescues where the animals are tended as well as the volunteer staff can manage—they are walked every day, they are examined by a dedicated medical staff, and they are given toys to play with and comfortable places to sleep. Sometimes I wonder if our loving smiles and voices are the first they've really known in some of their short lives. These people who care, employees and volunteers alike, work hard for the welfare of even the smallest animals, and I believe they are not only being good stewards of God's creation, they are displaying benevolence in action.

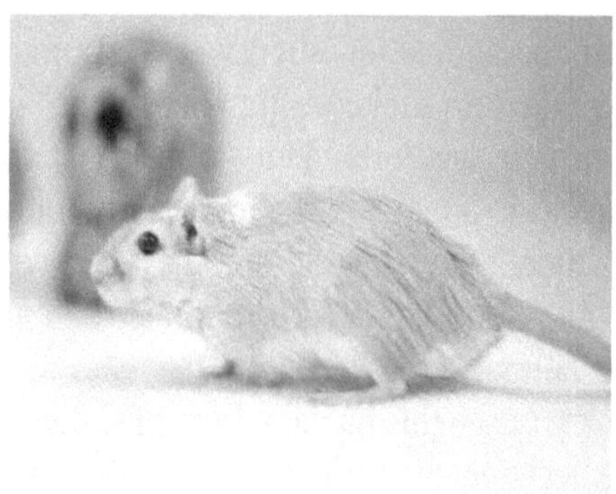

Pope John Paul II said, "A society will be judged on the basis of how it treats its weakest members, and among the most vulnerable are surely the unborn and the dying." I would add "and its animals" to that quote.

God cares for animals. Jesus said that God knew and noticed when a sparrow fell from the sky (Matt. 10:29). God was concerned even for the animals living in the wicked city of Ninevah (Jonah 4:11). Speaking through the prophet Hosea, God foretold of a day when "I will make a covenant for them with the beasts of the field, and with the fowls of heaven, and with the creeping things of the ground; and I will break the bow and the sword and the battle out of the earth, and will make them to lie down safely" (Hosea 2:18-19).

A few years ago I read a book that profoundly affected the way I think about mankind's relationship to the animal kingdom. The book was Dominion, by Matthew Scully, and I wish you'd read it, too. Scully is not a fanatic who would elevate animals above humans or even equate them, but he correctly points out that God gave man dominion over the earth, and as members of humankind we are His representatives. We stand in God's stead when we deal with animals, and do we desire for Him to treat us as we treat the animals within our circle of influence?

"I think their cries are noted," writes Scully. "As we often remind ourselves in other contexts, His ways are not our ways. There is, as the old hymn goes, a wideness in God's mercy greater than the mind of man. And who among us is so imbued with divine wisdom as to be certain that His mercy cannot reach down even to them? Here, more than anywhere, the animals can teach us a lesson in humility. Take man in all his glory, man in all his brilliance and power and conquests, and what are we to Him but what they are to us?"

As God cares about animals, so should we.

Americans have a lot of animals to care about—63 percent of American households have at least one pet, and that's seventy-one million homes. The SPCA estimates that nearly 79 million dogs and 86 million cats are owned in the United States. That's a good thing because "owned" pets live longer and healthier lives than strays.

Americans spend more money on their pets than any other civilized nation. In 2011, we spent over 50 billion dollars on our pets. Food and veterinary costs accounted for about 65 percent of that figure, but other pet services such as grooming, boarding, pet-sitting and pet hotels accounted for nearly four billion dollars. "Pet services" is the fastest-growing category of pet spending.

We pamper our pets, buying them toys, clothes, leashes, collars, pet bedding, and Christmas presents. We spend 26 billion annually for veterinary care and medicines, a fact that has persuaded many of us (including me!) to buy pet health insurance. With escalating costs in health care for everyone, pets included, no one wants to be forced to choose between helping their beloved pet or facing financial ruin.

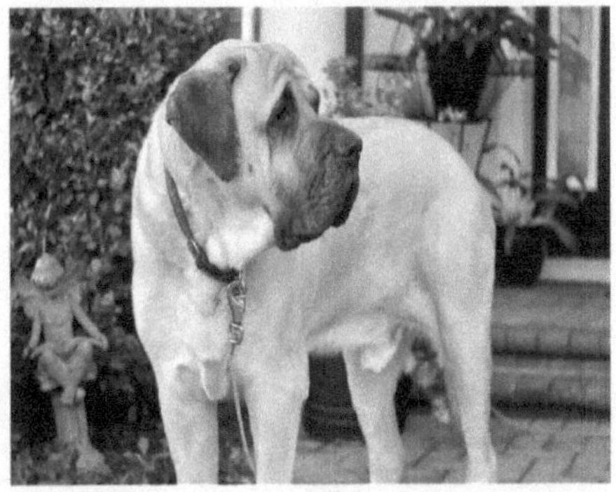

But not all pets are as well cared for as my dear Charley, pictured above. Thousands are abandoned or neglected every day, and others wander away from home and become lost because their owners didn't take the time to have the animal microchipped and/or secured safely. These animals might learn how to live on the street, but odds are that they will eventually be picked up and placed in an animal shelter. There they will either be adopted or humanely euthanized.

Approximately five to seven million companion animals enter animal shelters nationwide every year, while three to four million—more than half-- are euthanized (60 percent of dogs and 70 percent of cats). Shelter intakes are about evenly divided between those animals relinquished by owners and those picked up by animal control.

•According to the National Council on Pet Population Study and Policy (NCPPSP), less than 2 percent of cats and only 15 to 20 percent of dogs are returned to their owners. Most of these were identified with tags, tattoos or microchips.

•Twenty-five percent of dogs who enter local shelters are purebred. (Source: NCPPSP)

•According to the American Pet Products Association, only 10 percent of the animals received by shelters have been spayed or neutered, while 78 percent of pet dogs and 88 percent of pet cats are spayed or neutered. (Source: APPA).

•More than 20 percent of people who leave dogs in shelters adopted them from a shelter. (Source: NCPPSP)

What motivated me to work at my local animal shelter? Concern for animals, certainly. A love for dogs in particular. (I love cats, too, but I'm highly allergic to them).

Most of all, I believed I could do more good with my camera at a shelter than I could ever do with it sitting at home.

A New Movement Begins

The emphasis on better shelter animal photography may have started years ago, but I only became aware of it around 2011. Until a few months ago, most of the shelter websites I looked at featured dismal, blurred photos of frightened animals cowering behind bars or tethered by a leash to a hook on the wall. Nothing about those photos made me want to rush out and adopt an animal, though they did make me feel sorry for any pet unfortunate enough to end up in such a place.

But on a Sunday morning a few months ago I was getting ready for church when I happened to glance at the television. The program was CBS's "Sunday Morning," and the interview featured Teresa Berg, a professional photographer who volunteered to help a dachshund rescue group in Texas. While many shelter photographers believe that the most effective photos feature sad-eyed animals behind bars or fences, after seeing Teresa's work I came to believe that the most effective pictures feature animals who look loved, pampered, and perfectly at home on a fine piece of furniture.

After searching for more of Berg's photos on the Internet, I found pictures of dogs in pearls perched on carved chairs. I saw pit bulls with cashmere scarves wound around their necks. I saw perfectly ordinary dogs made to look extraordinary, not with elaborate costumes, but with simple adornments and well-chosen settings. And I thought, *I can do that. Or at least try to do something similar.*

So I sent an email to our local shelter and received a quick reply—they had lots of photographers, but they could use another volunteer. But I'd have to be trained first.

Trained? For a moment I was baffled. I've lived with dogs all my life, and I've had all kinds of dogs. I've read books on dog behavior, I've been to obedience classes, I once even hired a canine psychotherapist to help a shy/aggressive mastiff who joined our family.

But I soon realized that the training session had nothing to do with what I knew or didn't know about animals—it had everything to do with the way the shelter operated. To keep order, they have procedures that need to be followed. Those who volunteer also need to be able to answer basic questions posed by visitors.

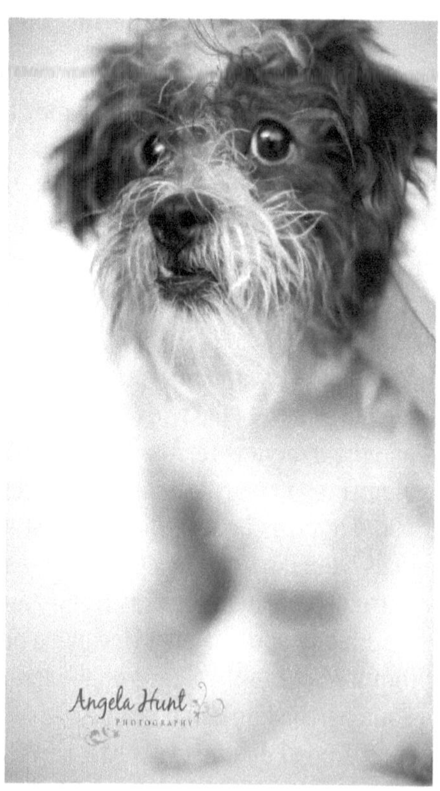

When I am wearing my SPCA shirt, the uniform of our volunteer staff, I am frequently stopped by visitors and asked about our available animals.

Fortunately, I can usually give them an answer or at least point them in the right direction.

During my training session, I learned how to handle the dogs (as in how to put on a Martingale collar), how to safely and securely get animals in and out of cages or kennels, and what to do if a dog should slip away from me. (When an athletic dog leapt over the bottom half of his kennel door and got away from me a couple of weeks later, I was glad I knew to yell "loose dog!" and happier still when another volunteer caught him.) I learned to wash my hands after handling one animal and before taking out another; I learned where the dangerous "bite zones" are and how to protect those areas if I ever found myself threatened by an animal.

To date, I have never felt threatened by a shelter dog. Most of them have been behavior tested by the time they are available for adoption and ready for their photo, so they're usually good with people. But I never assume that a dog is friendly, and I never push myself on a dog who is timid, shy, or nervous. When dogs perceive a threat, they will either flee or fight, so I give them lots of space to get away from me or the camera. I also avoid pressing on a dog's hindquarters, I scratch under their chins instead of bringing my hand down to pat their heads (nearly all dogs will flinch at that approach), and I avoid touching the sensitive stomach area—unless they roll over and beg for a belly rub.

During my training, I also learned how to transfer my completed photos over the web, how to label them for the shelter's use, and how to log in and out of two secure web sites—one for photos, the other for volunteer scheduling. I learned how to handle the paperwork, and how to indicate that a particular animal had been photographed—a considerate act, lest another volunteer photographer come along behind me and waste time re-snapping an animal.

I'll admit I was a little nervous when I went into the kennel to handle animals myself for the first time—and I'm a woman who lives with mastiffs, the heaviest, strongest dogs on the planet. In my earliest attempts I took too long to get the Martingale collars around the dog's necks, I couldn't figure out how to adjust the collars easily, and I was especially wary around the pit bull breeds—and there are a lot of pit bull breeds in shelters. But as I worked with the dogs, and as I got to know the bully breeds, I relaxed and fell in love with all my new furry friends. I have become an advocate for the pit breeds, and when I next find myself looking for a new dog to adopt, I may start with one like Vinny, pictured below. He was a sweetheart.

(It's a good thing my neighborhood has a two-pet limit, or I'd be in trouble.)

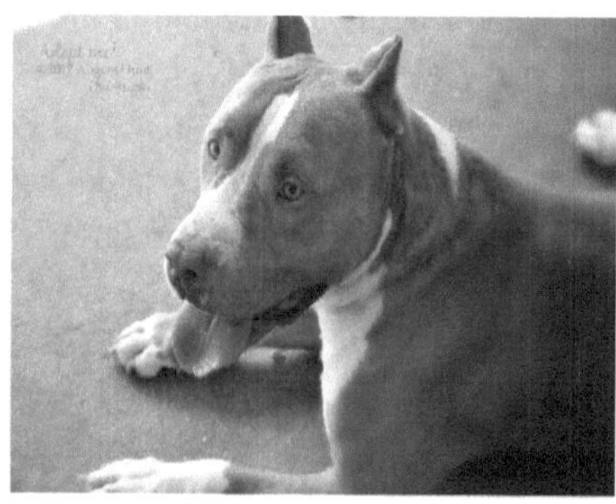

The pit breeds have a strong desire to please, and that's why they are so often used in illegal dog fighting. But that same strong desire can make a wonderful family dog, and in fact, the pit bull breeds were routinely used as babysitters around the turn of the century. Helen Keller had a pit bull that was her near-constant companion. I don't want to chase a rabbit trail, but if you're interested in learning more about pit bulls—and the shelters are full of them—you can start here.

In my work at the shelter, I've snapped photos of puppies and elderly dogs, small breeds, giant breeds, and just about everything in between. And I've loved them all. I think you'll love them just as much if you want to join in the adventure.

Photography Basics

First I'm going to assume that you are using a digital camera. Digital photography makes photographing animals easier because it's much less expensive than film. Last Thursday I photographed eight different animals and took over 1,000 shots to get twenty-four good pictures. If I were shooting those pictures on film, it'd cost a fortune and several hours to develop them. Hardly worth it, since some animals will be adopted even before the photos come back from the developer.

(Update: now that I've been doing this for several years, I don't take as many shots as I did in the beginning. I've learned to wait for the good shots, and now I average about thirty shots per dog—or less. If a dog is cooperative, this job is a breeze!)

I don't intend for this book to be a primer on digital photography because bookstores are filled with excellent books on the subject. You can also subscribe to wonderful online photography groups where you can learn from pros and feel free to ask questions of those with more experience. (My favorite is www.uglyhedgehog.com.)

But if you've never done a lot of photography, or if you've only taken snapshots for the family album, there are a few basic principles with which you should be familiar. You don't need a fancy camera to shoot photos for your animal shelter, but if you have a nice camera, you ought to know how to take advantage of the options it offers. I use a Nikon dSLR (digital single-lens reflex), and it took a while to master the many features available for my use.

Most point and shoot cameras produce perfectly lovely photos with good focus. Good focus, however, doesn't create a particularly artistic photograph. If you can blur the background and keep the foreground in focus, you'll create a shot that draws the viewer's eye to the object in the foreground. This concept of blurred backgrounds or surroundings refers to the **depth of field**, and it is greater when you shoot with a wide aperture, or shutter opening.

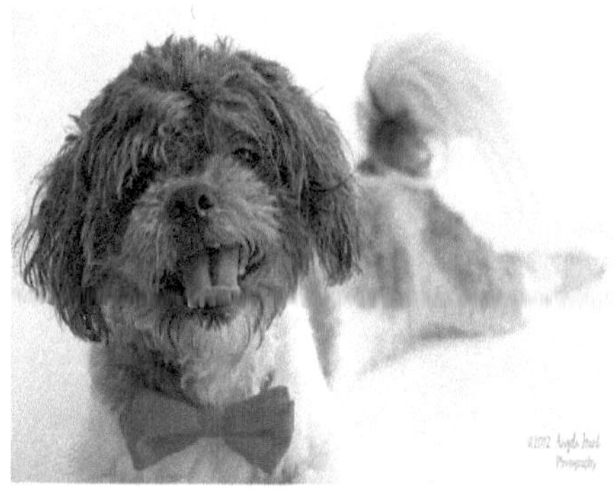

Consider the photo of Teddy above. See how his face and eyes are nice and sharp while his hindquarters and tail are slightly blurry or "soft?" That's the result of a shallow depth of field. You can see all of the dog, but your focus is directed toward his face, because I want you to notice his merry eyes and nice smile.

I also did a bit of work with Teddy's eyes. Because his hair prevented his left eye from catching the light, I painted in a tiny white dot for the light in his eyes. It's that little bit of shine in the eyes that makes an animal look lively.

Three settings on your camera determine how your image will look: the **ISO** setting, the **aperture** setting, and the **shutter speed**. The ISO corresponds to the ASA speed on older film cameras—the number indicates how sensitive the "film" is to light. There is no film in digital photography, but the ISO setting still refers to how sensitive to light the camera will be. If you're photographing in bright daylight, you set the camera on 100 or 200, a low ISO number. If you're shooting in a dark concert hall, you might set the ISO as high as 1600 or even higher. The higher the ISO setting, the less external light you will need to light the subject. But the higher the ISO setting, the more "noise" will appear in your picture. "Noise" is a sort of digital garbage that prevents the picture from being crystal clear. If you're hoping for a grainy, dated sort of look, noise can be a good thing. But most photographers keep the ISO setting as low as possible to avoid noise in their photos.

Understanding aperture

Try this experiment: sit in front of your computer and hold your index finger about six inches away from your face. Stare at your index finger. Without refocusing your eyes, look at your computer— the image on your monitor is blurry, isn't it? That's because you've focused on your finger, which is in the foreground.

Now curl your left hand into a ball so that you can place it up to your eye with only a tiny opening for light to pass through. Hold up your right finger so that you can see it through the opening in your curled left hand. Look at your finger—you can see the background screen in the distance, and this time it's not blurry, is it?

In the same way, when your camera has a tiny shutter opening—say, an aperture reading of 1/22, you will have a deep depth of field—and everything in the shot will be in focus. But if your camera has a large opening, such as when you didn't hold up your left hand at all, the object in the foreground will be in focus while the background will be blurred. This blurring is useful and quite artistic when you want to focus the viewer on the main object in the shot and not the unimportant or distracting background.

Naturally, if you position your subject right in front of a backdrop or object, you won't have room for much depth of field because your subject and the background are close together. But if you are shooting a person or an animal outdoors or in a field, you have the opportunity for wonderful depth of field. It will occur naturally if you shoot with a wide aperture (or small numbered F stop).

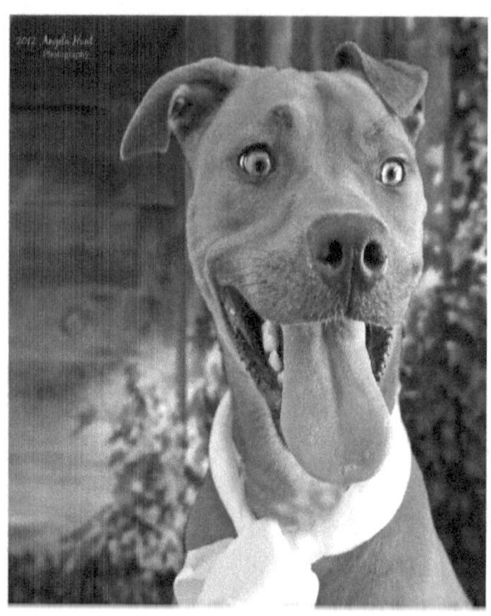

In your photo processing, if you ever need to "cut" your subject out of a photo and add a digital background (for instance, if your dog would not sit in front of your backdrop and posed instead in front of an ugly fence), you might want to blur the digital background to approximate a natural depth of field. For instance, in this photo of Lucy, originally taken against an ugly fence, I wanted to cut out the fence and substitute that lovely weathered barn. So I added a digital background, then blurred it so that the ivy and the boards appear soft. Then I added Lucy back into the photo. Now she appears to be sitting closer to the photographer while the barn remains in the background.

You can add a blurry depth of field in some photo processing programs, but I've found that it looks far more natural to let DOF come from the camera.

If you have a camera without interchangeable lenses, you can still take lovely artistic shots by using your zoom. Experiment with DOF by snapping pictures of your pets, flowers in your garden, or the neighborhood kids. See what kinds of effects you can render with your camera.

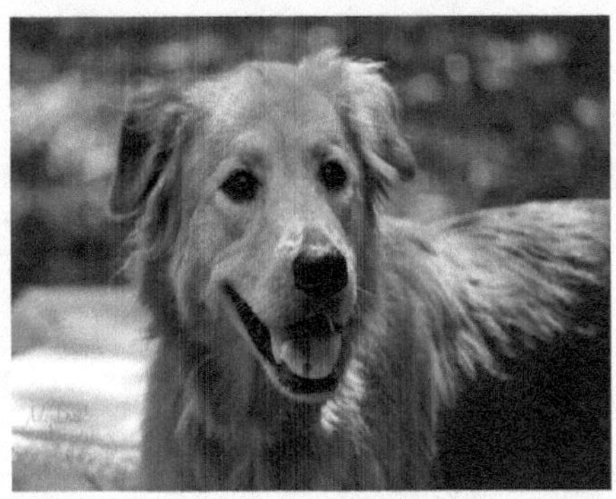

I remember the day I photographed Lola, pictured above. She was a beautiful Golden Retriever, one of my favorite breeds, but she was desperately nervous and shy. I tried to photograph her in my staged area, but she simply wouldn't sit—she wouldn't even stand still. The more I pursued her, the more nervous she became. So on a hunch, I walked her to a large fenced area at our shelter where the dogs can run and play. I released her, then removed my prime, non-moveable lens and put a zoom lens on my camera. I crouched down and took several photos of Lola as she forgot all about me. From a safe distance I was able to get gorgeous pictures of her while she ran, played, and frolicked in the little pool. Thanks to the zoom lens, I was able to get close-ups, and Lola wasn't traumatized in the least. As one of my photographer buddies says, "Her happy came out."

In the photo above, notice how Lola is in focus, while the background is blurred. That's depth of field. That's the effect of using a wider aperture. Who wants to look at the dried leaves in the background when you can study that beautiful dog?

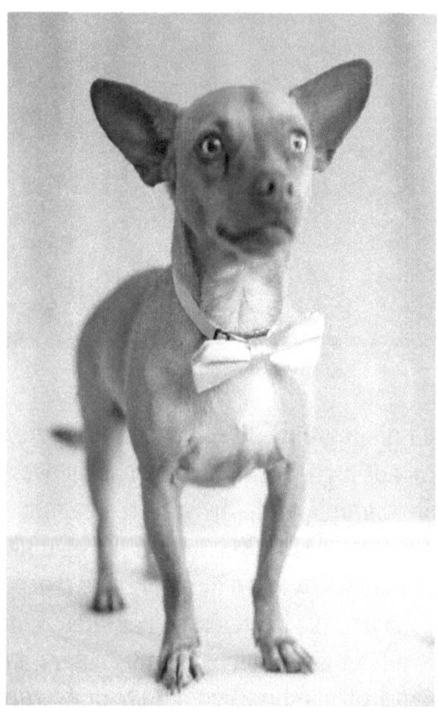

To summarize, the aperture setting determines how much light is allowed into the camera through the shutter opening. Think of the shutter as a pie—a big circle. Shutter settings are also referred to as F stops. A shutter setting of F4 is one-fourth of the pie, so it's a large opening. A shutter setting of F22 is only 1/22th of the pie, so it's a much smaller opening. It may be confusing, but the larger the F stop, the smaller the amount of light coming into the camera and the greater the depth of field. Think of looking through that tiny hole in your curled hand—everything was in focus, so you had a large depth of field through a tiny (large number) shutter opening.

Simplifying Shutter Speed

The third setting you need to understand is the shutter speed. This, of course, determines how long the shutter will be open and, logically, how much light will enter through the F stop opening. A shutter speed of 1/30 of a second is slow. If you are taking photographs of animals, you ought to have your shutter speed at least 1/250—that's quick, but still not quick enough to freeze a fast dog's movement. When I'm photographing dogs, I usually use a shutter speed of 1/500 or higher.

But when you cut down on the *time* light can pass through the aperture, you may have to increase that aperture in order to allow enough light for proper exposure.

Many cameras come with preset features—you can rotate a dial to "portrait" or "landscape" or even "pets." If you'd rather not worry about figuring out the proper shutter speed and aperture settings, these automatic modes may be perfect for you. The camera automatically decides which would be best for whatever you're shooting, and the results can be wonderful.

Most cameras come with several basic modes, though your camera may identify them by a different name:

•**Program** mode: fully automatic, the camera decides everything for you. But the result will be like a snapshot: everything in focus, no special effects.

•**A, or Aperture** mode: You decide which aperture you want to use (large or small), and the camera automatically sets the ISO and shutter speed for you, depending upon the available light.

•**S, or Shutter** speed mode: You decide which shutter speed you want to use (slower or faster), and the camera automatically sets the ISO and aperture for you, depending upon the available light.

•**M, or Manual** mode: you decide everything on your own. You use the camera's built-in light meter to adjust ISO, aperture, and shutter speed. Shooting in manual takes time and often requires a series of trial and error shots to get the desired effect. If you're in a hurry, this isn't the best mode to choose. If you're shooting a scene that might call for special settings, then manual is what you want to use.

Other modes your camera may offer include: portrait, landscape, child, sports, close up, night portrait, night landscape, indoor party, beach/snow, sunset/ dusk/dawn, pet portrait, candlelight, blossom, autumn colors, food, silhouette, high key (for bright subjects), and low key (for dark subjects). Each "scene mode" will automatically select ISO, aperture, shutter speed, and other options to give you the best possible picture. If you are just beginning to experiment with photography, these modes will help you achieve good photos faster than if you had begun to learn by shooting in manual mode.

Which mode do I shoot in? All of them. I like to experiment in manual mode, but if I'm short on time, or if my subject has reached the end of his attention span, I may switch to one of the automatic modes to get the shots I need. I rarely use program mode, however, because there's almost always a setting more appropriate.

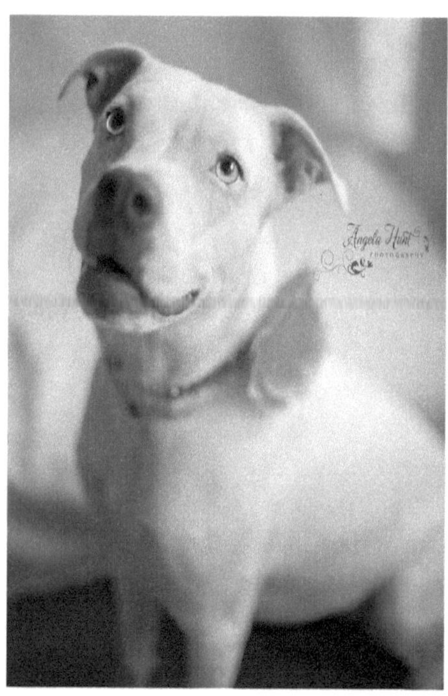

Focusing: Most digital cameras automatically focus a shot when you press the shutter button halfway. Many cameras will emit a beep when the photo is correctly focused, signaling that it's okay for you to go ahead and take the shot. Of course, many animals won't wait for you to focus and shoot, and many cameras have a "lag" time between the time you press the button and when the shutter actually opens. This is why I set my camera to **burst mode**, or **continuous**, when I'm photographing animals. This setting on the camera determines how a photo is taken—as a single shot, in a continuous burst, with the self-timer, or with a wireless remote. Just be aware, however, that burst mode is not available if you're using a flash because the flash needs time to recharge.

On many occasions I've framed a cute shot with my camera and pressed the button, only to have the dog or cat move at that exact second. But I keep my finger on the shutter, letting the camera click again and again, and I've been surprised by some of the darling shots I accidentally catch. You may never realize just how good—or bad—a shot is until you get it home and examine it on a large screen, but that's part of the fun. Sometimes we discover unexpected treasure!

I'd like to introduce one more topic while we're discussing photography techniques: **composition**. You may be inclined to put your subject in the very center of the shot, but resist that impulse if you can. Most pictures look better when composed according to "the rule of thirds"—in other words, when the subject lies along lines that mark the ⅓ or ⅔ points of the frame and not in the very center. These off-center shots are more interesting because they are a bit unexpected. As a novelist, I find that composition is like writing dialogue —characters' conversations are always more fascinating when people *don't* respond with the expected answer.

Don't worry if you get home and discover that you have a series of center-weighted shots—you can always crop them so your subject falls along better lines. More on that when we discuss processing your pictures.

When you're focusing your photo, however, most cameras default to focusing on objects in the center of the frame—so if your subject is off to the right or left, the camera may focus on something in the background, leaving you with a perfectly sharp background and a blurry subject. In order to prevent this, look through the viewfinder, position the subject in the center of the frame, and press your shutter button halfway to focus. Then, while still keeping the shutter button pressed halfway, move the camera frame a bit to the right or left, then press to take the picture. The subject will remain in focus and your composition will be improved.

Notice that Bridgette, in the portrait below, is slightly off center—look at her head, and see that there is more space between her right eye and the right margin than her left eye and the left margin. But I think the balance of her body, which is bottom right, balances out her left-situated head. Many photo processing programs supply grids for cropping, so you can line up the major elements in a photograph and crop according to the rule of thirds. But do what looks best to you.

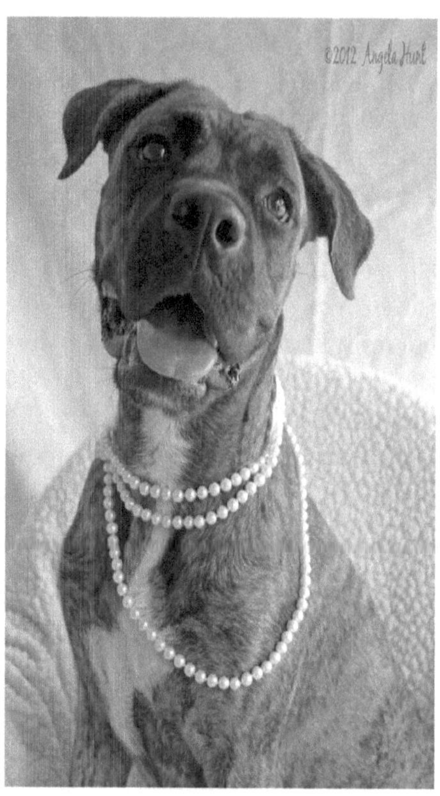

If your camera has a moveable focus point, always try to place that focus point on one of the subject's eyes. As viewers, we always look to the eyes first, so they need to be sharp and clear. If you simply point and shoot, your camera may focus on another prominent point—the nose. I have dozens of nose-focused photos, and while they might be useful if I want to do a study of nostrils one day, they don't make the best animal portraits. So either use a smaller aperture (higher number) so that both are in focus, or focus on the eyes, then shift the camera while still holding the shutter halfway down so the camera will hold that focus setting. Then snap. Works like a charm.

While you're taking pictures, get into the habit of glancing at your digital screen and checking the last few shots you took. You won't be able to see much detail in the pictures unless you zoom in, but you will be able to tell if the exposure is drastically off. Sometimes I'll be working with the camera set on "pet portrait" and my finger will accidentally move the dial toward "candlelight." I wouldn't realize my mistake if I didn't glance at my pictures every once in a while and notice that the exposure had changed.

Most digital cameras offer you an option on the type of photo files you'll receive when you upload your shots to the computer: most photographers shoot in jpeg (or .jpg) and that's a perfectly practical option. Jpeg files are easy to transfer and don't take up a great deal of space on your memory card or in your computer. But the camera has to do some processing in order to compress the image into a jpeg file, so it "drops" a lot of the colors and details in the pixels.

Lately I have begun to shoot in the raw format, and I don't think I'll ever go back to jpegs. The files are much larger, meaning that I can't get as many shots on my memory card, but since I delete shots from my card once I upload them to the computer, this hasn't been an issue.

So why bother with shooting raw images? Because when shooting in raw, the camera does absolutely no processing, preserving all the details and colors the camera picked up. You can then process the photo yourself, adjusting the white balance, color, and exposure, and noise level. When the photo looks the way you want it to, you can then save it as a Photoshop image and post-process in your favorite post-processing program. This can be a huge advantage if you snap several photos without checking on your camera settings—if you've shot several images that are severely over- or underexposed, you can probably salvage the shot if you shot it in raw.

This chapter is only a basic introduction to photography, but if you want to know more, I suggest you first study your camera's manual (yes, they are meant to be read) and read _Dog Photography for Dummies,_ by Kim Rodgers and Sarah Sypniewski. The latter book contains all kinds of useful information and is a great resource if you want to go deeper into photography and pet photography in particular.

CHAPTER
4

Working at the Shelter

As you begin to work at your local animal shelter, keep in mind that they have guidelines and you need to abide by them. Go to your training session, and learn how to properly handle the dogs. Follow the rules for keeping things clean. Scoop poop if your subject takes a potty break. Respect the other volunteers and try to make things easier for them. At my shelter, we're taught not to remove a dog from a kennel if there's another dog coming toward us, or if there are other people (especially children) about. When we're taking dogs out for a photo, we lead them out of the kennel as quickly as possible in order to avoid any contact or aggression with the other animals, even those in kennels.

During my training, an experienced volunteer told me a story that made me shudder: once a volunteer took a dog out and it promptly attacked a dog across the aisle. That dog's feet were sticking out beneath the kennel gate, and the leashed dog mangled the kenneled dog's feet so badly that in the end, both dogs had to be put down. A terrible tragedy, and a story I'll never forget.

When you begin to work at the shelter, remember that others have come before you. Other photographers have been working there for months or years, and their style may not be like yours. Each photographer will have his or her own way of taking pictures, and yours is not better or worse, it's simply different.

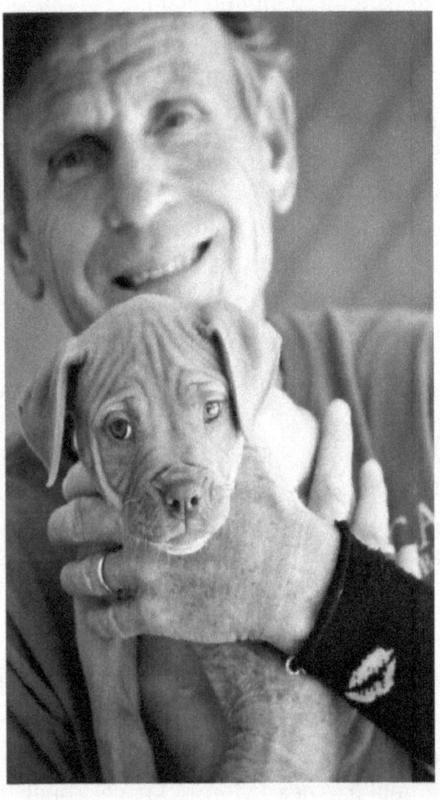

When I began, a veteran photographer, Jim McCook, took me under his wing and helped me find my footing. Jim's specialty is catching unexpected shots with the dogs outdoors—dogs nosing horses, frogs landing on a dog's head, and action shots of dogs frolicking in the pool. I wanted to try something different (pearls and feather boas and such), but Jim never criticized, he simply helped me find my way around and we worked together. We still work together quite often, and I admire his dedication. When he's not taking pictures, he's at the shelter several times a week to walk the dogs. He's also a dedicated fundraiser.

So when you meet the other photographers, don't feel threatened or insecure, just jump in and do photography the way you envision it. Just remember to keep the emphasis on the animal—no technique or prop or effect should overpower the animal's spirit.

At our shelter, we sign up for a particular day, and can photograph any animals who are available for adoption and haven't already been photographed. We don't take pictures of animals who are still in the medical wing, and we don't take photos of animals who aren't available yet for some reason. Better for all concerned if we wait until the animals are officially ready to be adopted.

Shooting at the animal shelter can be a challenge in terms of finding a proper space. Lighting is a major consideration, especially if you are shooting outdoors in hard sunlight or indoors under fluorescent bulbs. If you're fortunate, you'll be able to find a small room or fenced area where you can let the dog roam freely and not have to worry about removing a leash and/or unattractive collar from the picture during post processing. At our shelter, cats are always kept inside, and we can photograph them in one of several small rooms. Ditto for bunnies and pocket pets like mice and hamsters.

If you're shooting indoors, of course, you will probably need a flash or other supplemental lighting source. If you're shooting outdoors, look for a shaded and fenced area. You'll find it helpful if this area is away from the other dogs, so your subject isn't distracted by the sounds, sights, and smells of the other animals.

By the time an animal is ready for adoption, she has probably already been at the shelter for a week or longer. During that time she has undergone a medical exam, spaying if she wasn't already fixed, and a behavioral evaluation. If the animal had heart worms, kennel cough, or some other illness, she may have been held in the medical wing until her treatment was completed.

New arrivals in the adoption area may be frightened, confused, or unhappy when a photographer comes to get them for their photo session. Unhappy or nervous animals do not want to smile for the camera, so the best photo may be one of a dog with sad eyes. Fortunately, these photos can tug at the heart strings, so they may be perfectly suitable for your shelter's website.

While I was learning the ropes, I took photos in several different locations. I liked the indoor "real life room" we use to see how dogs behave in a non-kennel environment, but that room was often occupied when I arrived and therefore unavailable. I shot in the puppy play pen for a while, but that area was covered by sand and gravel. The dogs tended to kick up dust when they ran and played, resulting in a dirty dog and photographer (plus I worried about dust and sand getting into my camera).

Jim suggested a spot that proved to be perfect. The place had been previously used as a rabbit pen—it had a concrete floor, which we routinely sweep, a roof that allows us to work in the rain and keeps us out of the hot sun, and four high walls, two fairly solid and two of chain link. If we had an unlimited budget, we'd cover those walls in a pretty painted backdrop, but the chain link allows a breeze to reach us—and trust me, in the midst of a scorching Florida summer, every whisper of wind is welcome.

So Jim and I have dubbed the old rabbit pen "The Pho-DOG-graphy Studio," and it's been a good place for us. For a nice-looking backdrop, I went to a local fabric store and bought three yards of different materials. I tried a white felt at first, but bright sunlight made the chain link fence visible through the backdrop. Then I bought machine washable craft fur in black and white, and those fabrics have worked well. They don't wrinkle, they don't reflect light, and they roll easily onto the big cardboard tubes my fabric store is usually willing to give me. (The sun occasionally shines through the white fur, so sometimes I have to hang another fabric over the back to increase the background's opacity.) Plus, craft fur is machine washable, which is important if a dog decides to pee on your photography setup.

Once I got the fabric home, I used my sewing machine to sew a "sleeve" for the cardboard tube by folding over the top five inches and sewing a straight seam. The backdrop stays nice and wrinkle free when in storage. When I'm ready to use it, I could mount the roller onto a backdrop stand, but at the shelter I prefer to simply unroll the fabric and drop the sleeve with the cardboard tube over the top of a tall fence. The weight of the tube holds the fabric in place while I'm shooting and a couple of clips secure the backdrop to the fence if the day is breezy.

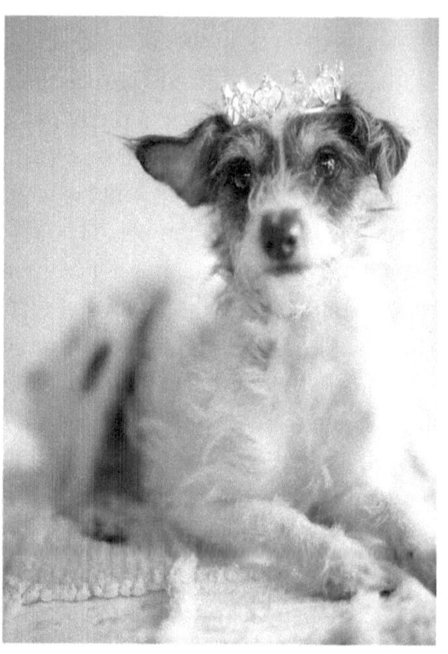

I've also found good backdrops in discount stores like Marshall's and T.J. Maxx. Shower curtains, often found in the clearance bin, make great backdrops and come with grommets at the top so you can use shower curtain hangers to hook them onto a fence. Look for neutral colors in a solid fabric—a busy print would overpower the animal you're trying to photograph.

I have also experimented with—and enjoyed—using cardboard project boards as backgrounds. Because these project boards (often used for students' science projects) are usually between three and four feet tall, they work best for smaller dogs. But their stark white surfaces are smooth and the final look is polished. At first I used a simple piece of white foam board as the base, but the dogs seemed to feel uncomfortable on its slick surface, so now I use a yard of white tee shirt material.

Whatever I use, I need to be sure it's clean for the next dog. Why am I a stickler for cleanliness? Because diseases like Parvo and kennel cough can spread like wildfire through a shelter, often with fatal results. To keep things as sanitary as possible, I use a fresh piece of fabric as the "flooring" for each dog—sometimes I may use a shiny piece of satin, a remnant of pleather, or something soft like fleece. After I've finished one dog's photos, I remove that piece of fabric and spread out another for my next subject. After the shoot, I gather up all the fabrics and take them home for laundering. Inexpensive fabric remnants of at least three-quarters of a yard are perfect to serve as "flooring" in a photo shoot, and you can choose colors to compliment the dog's coloring.

If too much sunlight streams in through any part of the fence, I can clip a thin piece of fabric to the chain link (I use an old white tablecloth) and it becomes a diffuser for the strong sunlight. Remember—"hard light"—any light that casts a strong shadow—is not your friend. Better to shoot in the shade.

All in all, the old rabbit pen has given us a perfectly lovely space. I hope you find such a place at your local shelter.

The Photo Shoot

Okay, so you have a dog waiting in a kennel and a camera around your neck. You have stashed your equipment and props in a safe and secure place. What do you do next?

You go meet your dog and take him out of the kennel. Some dogs will behave as if they want to be your best friend, and others will be so eager to get out of the building that they'll practically drag you down the aisle and out the door. But some dogs may be frightened and others may be shy. Some may even be aggressive due to their fear.

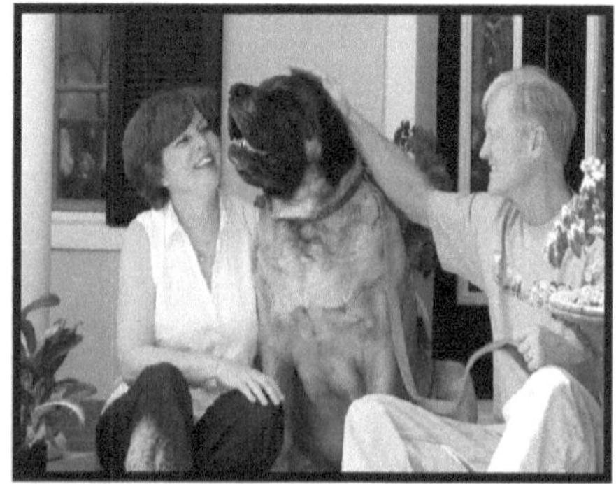

If you are male, be aware that some dogs are frightened by men. I'm not sure why—probably because of men's deep voices and larger stature, or perhaps they have unpleasant memories associated with male figures. One of my mastiffs, Babe, shown above, was a rescue who came from a mechanic's garage where she was kept on a chain all day. Because the majority of people she saw were men—and because dogs on a chain cannot flee, so they learn to respond with aggression—Babe was never happy when strange men approached our home. She took nearly a month to warm up to my husband and son, but she continued to bark ferociously at the UPS man every time he appeared at our door. She broke our glass front door once, and our dining room windows. All in an attempt to protect us from the fearsome UPS man. Women, however, she adored.

When the male vet at our animal hospital had to see Babe, he spoke in a soft, high voice. His willingness to do so eased Babe's fears and made the examination much easier.

So if you're male and you see signs of fear from a dog, switch into falsetto mode. Speak in a high, soothing voice, and be gentle. No matter what your gender, because dogs can regard direct eye contact as intimidating, don't look directly into the dog's eyes, but look at the top of his or her head as you slip on the leash and collar. This will enable you to see what's going on, but the dog won't think you're trying to challenge or intimidate.

If the dog is a puppy or elder dog, be careful when removing him from the kennel. If the dog is collar resistant—he refuses to allow his head to enter the circle of a collar—thread the link end of leash through the loop at the other end and then slip the resulting loop around the dog's head. You'll be able to tighten this enough to lead the dog out of the kennel. Just be sure to loop the single end around your hand so you don't lose the leash if the dog jerks you forward.

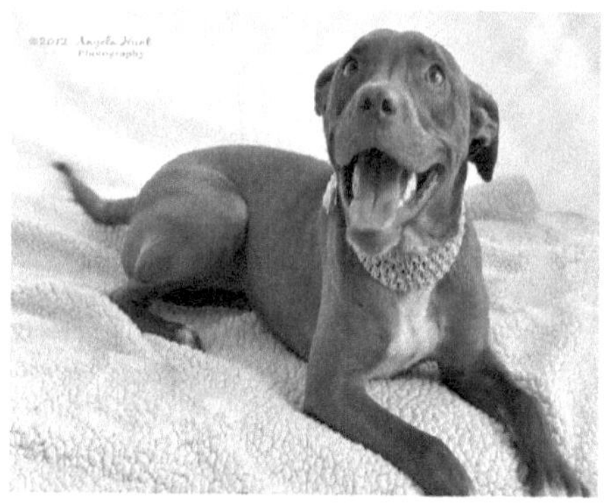

Once I have the dog firmly in hand, I walk my subject to our little studio, allowing him to sniff and explore and, if necessary, to relieve himself on the way. Then I use my happy voice and walk him to my small enclosure.

Once we are safely inside, the first thing I do is release the animal from the collar and leash I used to lead him out of his kennel. Our shelter also uses band collars that are a bit like hospital bracelets, and those I do *not* remove—they're meant to remain on the animal until he is adopted, and they contain information like his registration number and his sex. The dog's gender is important—you don't want to dress a male dog up in pink ribbon or put in female dog in a neck tie. (Confession: I have done both. These popular gender-neutral names can be confusing!)

While the dog scampers around and explores our space, I set up the shot. Depending on my subject's gender, breed, and coloring, I decide what sort of backdrop to hang, what sort of adornment I might use, and if I want him to sit in a basket, on a stool, or simply on the low platform Jim and I managed to commandeer from the medical unit's trash pile. (I think it's the padded top from an old examination table). I hang a backdrop to cover the unsightly chain link fence and choose a fabric to use as "flooring" for the shot. I pay careful attention to the dog's color—if he's a white dog, I will probably use my black background, and if he's a black dog, I will either use my white background or make sure I have lots of additional light. If he's a gray dog, I like to use red as the fabric flooring or perhaps a red bow tie. If the dog is brown and white, I may use a tan or beige blanket as the base. If the dog is a solid color, I may use a print, but if he's spotted, I'll probably chose a solid fabric.

I keep a box of baby wipes handy, but sometimes it's easier to remove eye gunk and dandruff while post processing the photo than clean a nervous dog's face. I still remember how cornered and uncomfortable I felt as a child when my mother approached me with a wet washcloth, so I can imagine how the dogs feel!

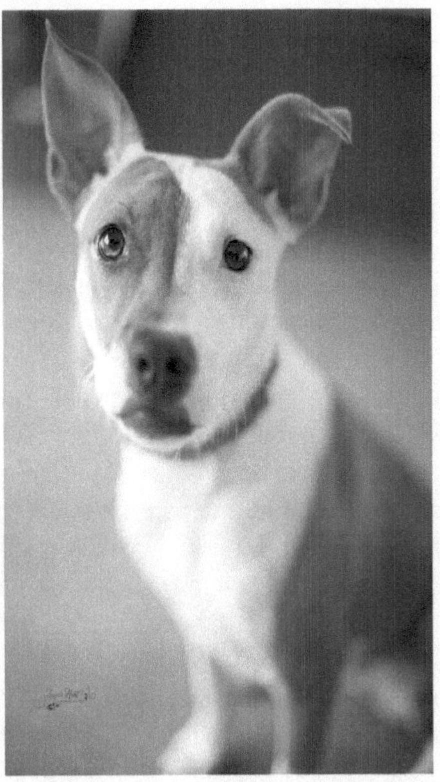

When I've set up, I stoop or sit on the floor to pet him for a while and speak softly to him. With some boisterous big dogs, I know better than to sit—some dogs can literally knock you over and pin you down with love taps and kisses. As a woman who lives with mastiffs, I know I'm asking for trouble if I lie on the floor—I'll be so overpowered by affectionate dogs that I might not make it up again!

Whenever I speak to the dog, I try to use his name. Puppies and strays may not recognize their names, having just received one at the shelter, but older dogs will certainly know and recognize the familiar sound of their name. And though a stray may not recognize the name a shelter has given him, any dog who has been through any kind of training is likely to recognize "Good boy!" or "Good girl!" When the dog does what you want him to do, praise him lavishly.

Even if the dog doesn't understand a word you say, he will certainly pick up on your approving tone of voice, so speak often. I'm probably unaware of the things I say because I talk now from habit, but the other day I got a kick out of listening to Jim photograph a dog. He croons to his subjects, saying things like "You are the prettiest girl, and the sweetest thing . . ." and the dogs lap up his attention. Praise, praise, praise when the dog does what you want him to do, and give him mild verbal corrections when he's off base.

I want my subject to relax and have fun while we are together—a happy dog takes a better picture. I call him by his name to see if he recognizes it. Then I take out a small treat and a toy, and offer both to the dog. This is important—I've discovered that some dogs are treat-motivated, and others are more toy-motivated. A few dogs, of course, are so nervous that they're not willing to be motivated by anything. With my left hand I hold either the treat or the toy—whichever the dog prefers—and ask him to sit. If he does, my work just became a thousand times easier. If he doesn't, I try to teach him to sit by touching the treat to his nose and then lifting it straight up. Most dogs will follow the treat with their eyes while their rear ends lower in a sit. If that doesn't happen, I might press lightly on the dog's hindquarters to see if he can grasp the idea. If he still resists, I decide to follow his whims and see what he will do.

I usually try to get the dog to sit or stand on the spot I've prepared. Most dogs will, especially if they're older dogs who have come from a home and understand what "sit here" means. Ideally, the dog will go to the spot I'm patting with my hand, he'll sit or stand, and I'll begin to snap pictures. I love smiling pictures, because they reveal how happy the dog is. I "bait" the dog with either the treat or the toy, whichever he prefers, by holding it over my head. If that causes the dog to lift his neck so high that I lose sight of his eyes, I lower the treat to my eye level or even set it on the top of my head. But no matter what, I try to take photos *at the dog's eye level*. On rare occasions, usually with a dog who's so lively he's likely to knock me over, I have stood over a dog and gotten a cute "heads up" shot like the one below. But that's only one shot, and I need at least three, so I have to find a way to get down to his level.

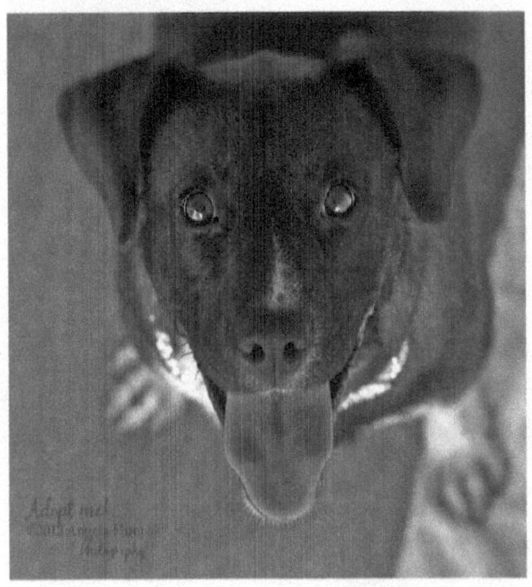

Sometimes I've asked an assistant to help by baiting the dog and found that if the helper holds the treat or toy too high, all we see of the dog in the resulting photo is neck. I want the dog's gaze to remain straight, so now I ask assistants (if I have one) to hold the treat or toy right above my head—or better yet, at my eye level. Sometimes an assistant can be of more help by holding an external flash or a reflector.

You don't have to have an assistant—in fact there's nothing more distracting to a dog than having TWO people trying to get his attention. You can usually handle the photo session alone—with one hand you wave the toy or treat and with the other you snap the picture. I work alone 99.9 percent of the time, and now I'm used to handling the camera with one hand and the toy or treat with the other.

I usually take at least twenty photos of each cooperative dog—in continuous mode, the shots add up quickly. Most of them will end up on the proverbial cutting room floor, but among them I often find some unexpected treasures. My shelter's web hosting service allows us to post three photos of each animal, so I usually try to get one standing shot, one sitting shot, and one close-up, but that's only an elusive ideal. It's more important that I get three *good* shots, and if the dog is sitting in all of them, that's fine. I am looking for photos—even goofy ones—that reveal the animal's personality.

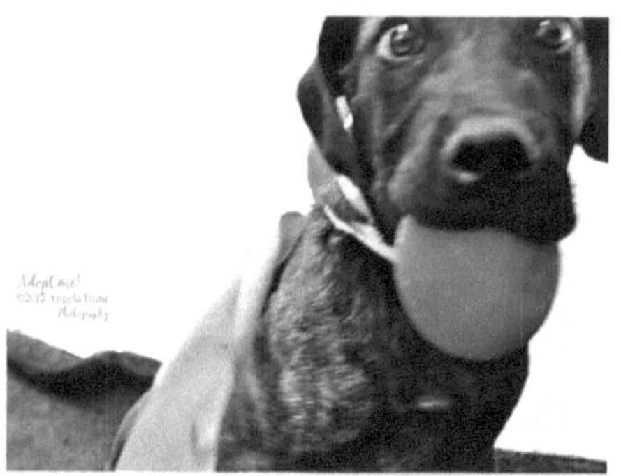

The above photo of Ringo is not particularly good—for one thing, it's blurry and his bow's untied. But I love it because of the guilty look in his eyes.

Know Your Subject

I've encountered several different kinds of dogs (and cats) during my time as an animal photographer, and here are some insights to handling them. These may also serve as a guideline for cats, but with cats, all bets are off. They do what they want to do.

1. **The cuddle bug.** Some dogs love people so much that all they want to do is climb into your lap. You can position them in front of your backdrop, but as soon as you lean back and remove your hand from their bodies, they try to leap into your arms. Sometimes even treats and toys don't hold them in position because these sweet dogs value human affection above everything else.

So how do you handle them? This is a good time to call for help. See if you can get a helper to sit with the dog in front of the background. Take the picture with the dog leaning against the helper, but fill the frame with the dog. Later, while post processing, you can crop out your assistant.

The beautiful boy below, Duke, had already caught the attention of his future adopters when I led him out to be photographed. The young couple wanted to see the dog, so, not wanting to hinder an adoption, I allowed them to come into the fenced area with me. Duke was so hungry for affection that he wanted to be petted by all three of us, so I had the young man sit in front of the backdrop and hold Duke steady while I snapped the photo. I could have cropped out more of the human, but I had a feeling that they were all going home together in a matter of minutes. Even so, the photo's focus is on the dog, not the human.

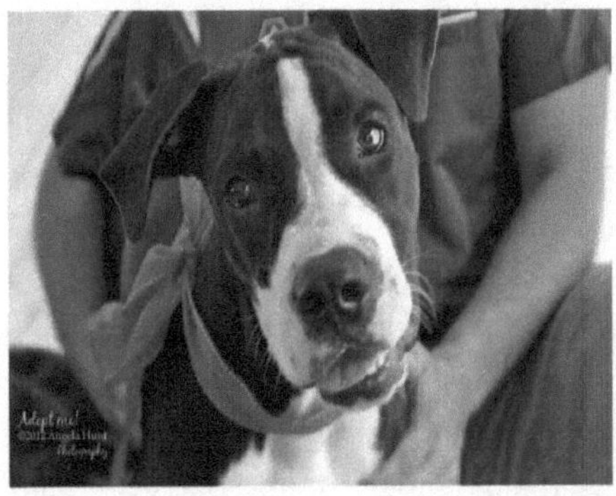

Another method to steady an attention-starved dog is to put him, if small enough, in a chair or on a table. Keep one hand on him while you frame the shot, then quickly lift your free hand and snap. You'll have to be quick, or the dog will launch himself into your arms again, and you don't want him to fall. We've used this technique with wiggly, scrambling puppies—three or four volunteers will help me get the puppies into a basket or wheelbarrow, then I count to three. On "three," they all lift their hands and I snap. It takes many, many shots, but the results can be amazing.

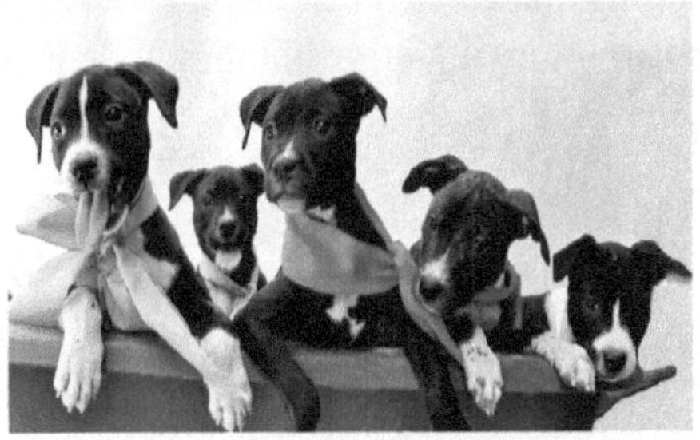

2. **The dog who fears the camera.** I haven't encountered too many dogs who are actually afraid of the camera, but when I meet one their fear is obvious. They are perfectly fine with me placing them in front of the backdrop, but the

moment I lift my camera, they turn their heads and look for a way to leave. To them the camera looks like a menacing black eye, and dogs are often intimidated by stares. So for these dogs, I use a zoom or telephoto lens and back away, giving them space so they feel more comfortable.

If I don't have another lens, I let them roam around the space at will while I wait for a moment to snap any happy shot from any location. I will probably blur the background in these shots, or cut out the background and use something else. The background isn't the important thing—the dog is.

3. **The dog who will not stand—or sit—still.** I don't often run into dogs that simply won't be still, but I've met a few. One was a Husky who was fascinated by something on the other side of the chain link fence—maybe a rat? A snake? I don't know what had been back there during the previous night, but this Husky obviously smelled something. He wouldn't come to me at all, he simply pawed and worried at that fence no matter what I did. Finally I resorted to a desperate action—I put him back into his collar and leash, then hooked the loop of the leash over a fence post. The Husky had no choice but to stand still—well away from the fascinating fence--so I got into position and quickly snapped a series of photos . . . while he stared at the back fence, of course. Later, I cropped out the leash.

The other day I photographed Honey, below, a sweet dog who was a bit nervous. She wouldn't stand still, either, and absolutely refused to remain on the nice padded surface in front of the backdrop. I offered toys and treats, but to no avail. So I simply sat there, relaxing in the sweltering heat of a Florida summer, until she grew tired of exploring and lay down. Fortunately, I had swept the floor so she was lying on a clean surface. I snapped several pictures from where I was sitting and we had our shots. Photos featuring a concrete floor as background aren't my favorite, but they'll do in a pinch.

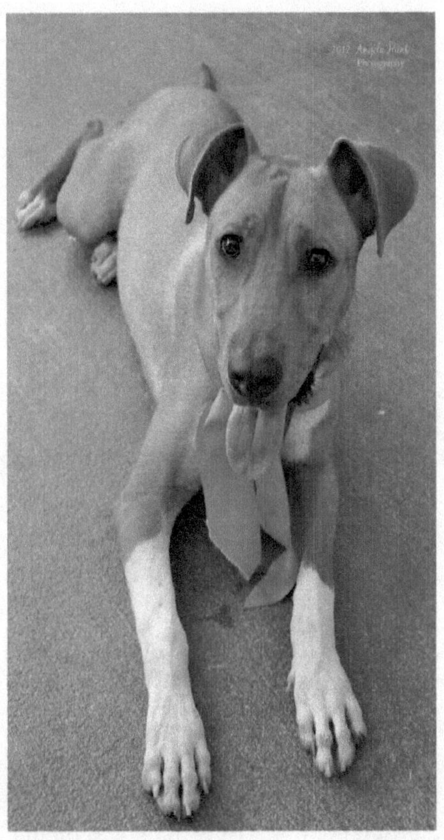

I also purchased a length of green "grass" indoor-outdoor carpet—ten dollars got me a strip about eight feet long and three feet wide. I keep it on the floor just for those occasions when a dog won't sit still. If he will lie down on the carpet, at least I'll have a nice, uncluttered shot.

4. **The dog who won't go near your backdrop.** Let's face it, dogs are curious and want to know about their surroundings. My backdrops must look like towering walls to them, and they're fascinated by all the sounds and scents outside those walls. I've had a few dogs who avoid my backdrops entirely and gravitate to the unattractive chain link fence, refusing to budge.

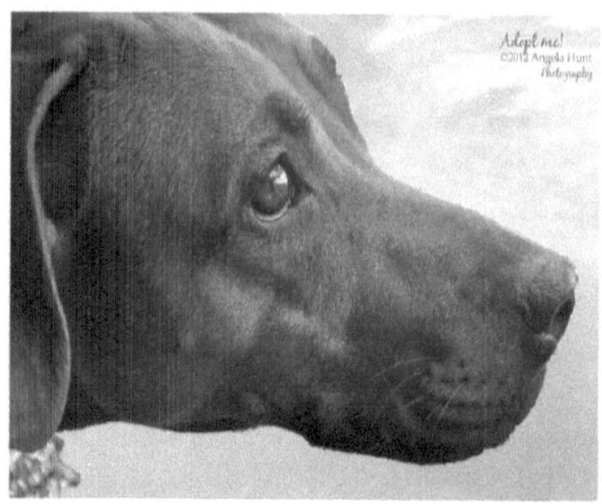

Well—no offense to folks who manufacture metal fencing, but chain link is not my idea of a beautiful background. I've experimented with several digital ways to erase the fences, and have come to rely on a little Photoshop magic. I simply erase the fence as best I can, and substitute a more interesting background—and something within the realm of possibility (I wouldn't, for instance, use a background with fairies and elves. At least I don't *think* I would.) Daisy, pictured above, was one of those dogs who wanted to keep her nose pressed to the fence, so I removed the fence and inserted a cloudy sky. She might look a little like a flying Superdog, but at least she's not peering through a chain fence.

I've also had dogs who will not sit or lie down on the lovely fabric "flooring" I've prepared, but will plop onto the floor and grin at me. I shoot the picture anyway, grateful that the concrete floor, while not the most attractive thing in the world, is better than dirt or gravel. It's a background. Olive Oil, below, didn't want to sit on my prepared space, but because she parked herself between the fabric and the green carpeting, I was able to get a shot.

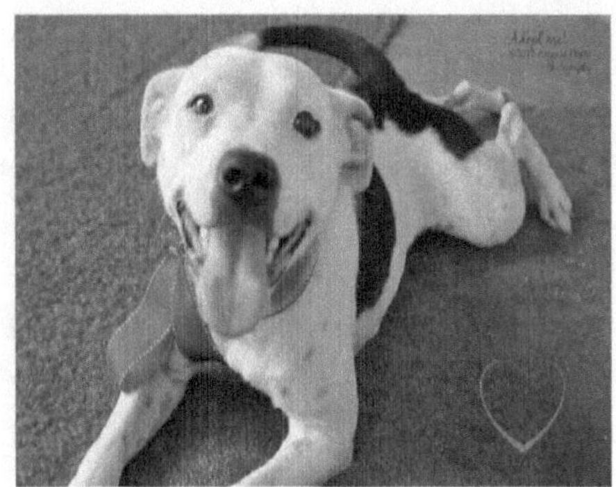

5. **The dog who will not look you in the eye.** They're rare, but they exist—those independent, wary types who simply don't want to cooperate and give you a direct smile. So they turn their aloof gaze anywhere but on you or your camera. Fine. Those handsome guys and gals can still produce a beautiful picture with a profile shot. Shoot their pictures anyway, and feature their profiles in your photos.

6. **The dog who will not perk up.** If I could only have two features in a picture, I would want alert eyes and erect ears. Dogs speak an entire language with their ears, and when a dog is alert his ears are forward and the look is beautiful. So how do you get a relaxed dog to perk up his ears? One way is to startle him with a new sound.

Every photographer has his or her own favorite sounds. I took a workshop from a professional photographer whose sound was—well, it's hard to describe. He roared. So loudly that I nearly jumped out of my skin. The sound was like all the vowels run together, and I don't think I'll ever be tempted to use it. I'm not even sure I could reproduce it.

My sounds are simple: I've discovered that dogs respond to the sounds of puppy whining, kitty meowing, and short, abrupt barks. Those often elicit quizzical looks and upright ears. When my vocal sounds fail, I resort to a squeaky bulb that I carry in a pouch hung around my neck. (The squeaky bulb came from a dog toy that didn't last long.) When that fails, I blow on a tiny harmonica that photographer Jim gave me—it, too, hangs from the lanyard I wear when taking pictures. Jim attaches a squeaky to his camera strap, so a noise maker is always within reach.

Dogs *do* respond to strange noises, but any noise is only effective two or three times. After that, the noise is no longer unique, so you'd better move on to something else. It's a great idea to develop your own repertoire of sounds, and use them without embarrassment. After all, we all do it.

If, after whining and squeaking and humming and singing, your subject will not perk up, go ahead and celebrate his laid back disposition. After all, some people are phlegmatic, so why should we be surprised to learn that some dogs are, too? I remember taking pictures of Korra—I think she was still a bit hung over from her spaying operation the day before, so I gently coaxed her to cooperate. And after all my efforts, I learned that "laid back" can result in an adorable photo.

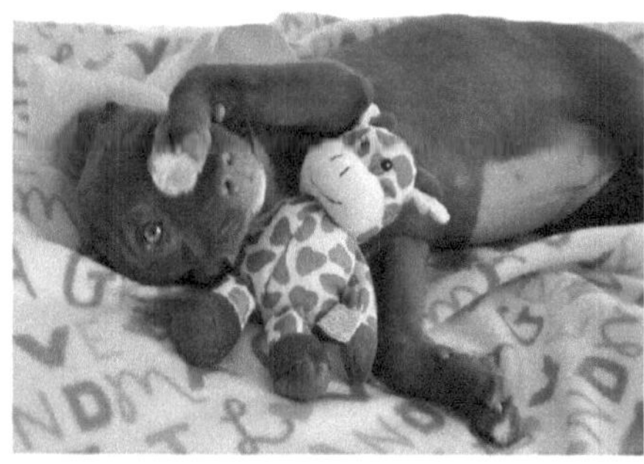

7. The dog with the mile-long tongue. I run into the tongue problem fairly frequently because we're in Florida, we usually photograph outdoors, and it's doggone hot. Dogs cool themselves by panting, and when they pant, out comes the tongue. Well, I don't know about you, but I don't find a long, fleshy tongue all that attractive, and I've caught dozens of them on film.

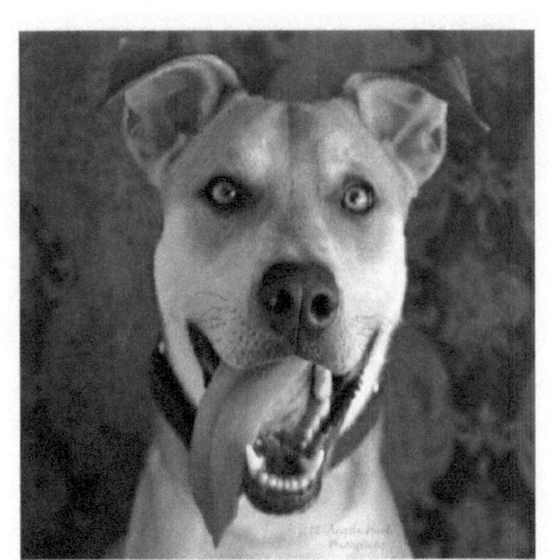

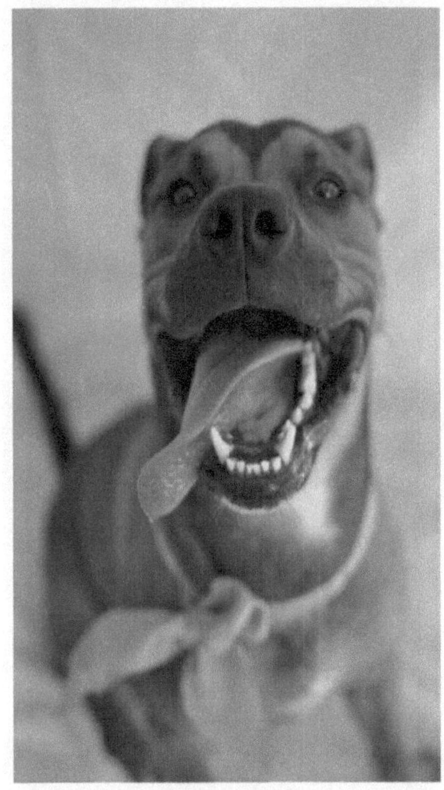

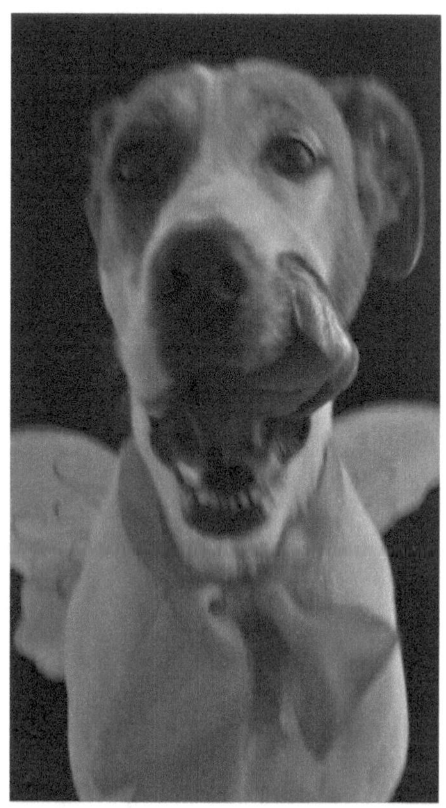

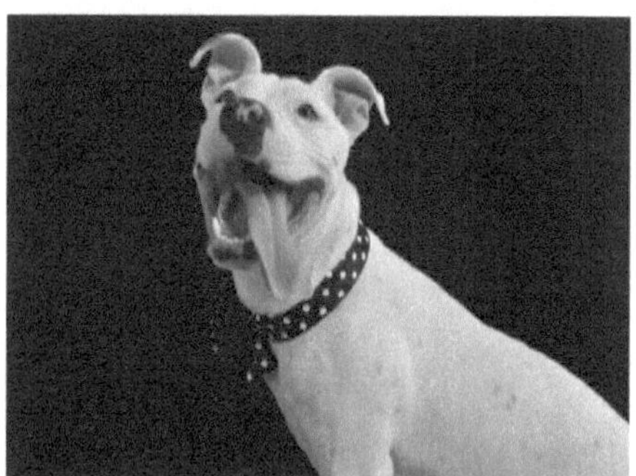

How do you get that tongue back into the dog's mouth? You might think to give a dog a drink of water, but that's no guarantee, and you'd also have the problem of dogs sharing germs unless you emptied and cleaned the water bowl after every photo session. I recently read that one photographer suggested spritzing the dog's tongue with lemon juice mixed with water, but frankly, I don't have enough hands to hold a camera, a squeaky, *and* a spritz bottle. What I usually do is rely upon the strange noise—if it's strange enough, the dog will often close his mouth and cock his head. If that doesn't work, I try the tiny dog biscuit. If I place a small treat on the blanket, the dog will eat it, lick his lips, and close his mouth, if only for a few seconds. That's when I grab my closed-mouth shots.

8. **Black dogs and cats.** If you've been involved in shelter work for any time at all, you've undoubtedly heard that black animals are the last to be adopted and the first to be euthanized. The so-called "black dog syndrome" may be attributed to many things—the idea that black animals are bad luck, the fact that most "mean" dogs in movies are black, and the reality that black animals are hard to photograph. If you leave your camera on its automatic settings, the resulting photo may be a black blob with appendages.

Photographer Seth Casteel of Little Friends Photo in Los Angeles says any shelter pet can pose a photo challenge, but black ones top the list. "I hear about Black Dog Syndrome all the time," Casteel told *USA Today*. A bad picture can make a pet look sick, mysterious or even ominous, he said. "To photograph a black dog or cat effectively, you want to capture personality, important physical traits and details and have the photo be in focus. The key is lighting and shutter speed."

To photograph a black dog, don't put him in bright sunlight, which only throws dark shadows onto a dark dog. Put your subject in the shade, and increase your shutter speed. When digitally processing the photo, you may want to overexpose the photo until you can see the texture of the dog's fur. You want to avoid the "black blob" look even if it makes the animal appear slightly gray.

You can also make a black dog more appealing by giving him a bit of bright decoration—a bright silk flower at his neck, a colorful silk ribbon, or a jaunty bandana.

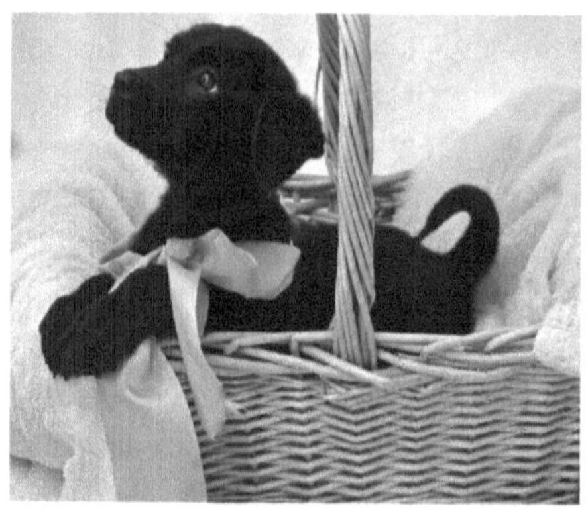

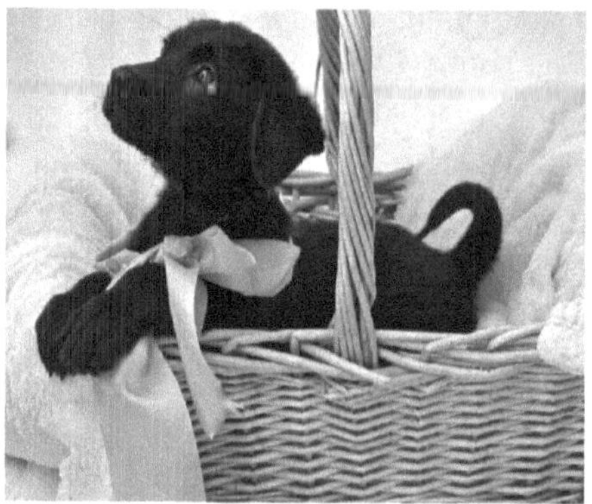

In the first photo of puppy Miles, one of my early efforts, his fur looks like a solid black mass. I edited the second photo again, brightening the shadows until I could see individual hairs on Miles's ear and paws. I also sharpened the photo a bit. Both steps help prevent the "black blob" problem when photographing a black cat or dog.

Photographing Felines

Snapping cats at the animal shelter can be a challenge in terms of finding a proper place to set up, especially if you're photographing during the spring or summer, when there are lots of kittens that need homes. I remember one day in July when I showed up with a backdrop, lights, and everything I needed for a professional looking shoot, but when I went into the cat wing,

every single room was taken up with cats. The volunteers had been reduced
to using a hallway as a "get acquainted room" for cats and prospective new
owners, so I had no place to put all that equipment.

I went home that day, but went back on a Saturday, which are always
busy days at the shelter. Because we had so many cats who needed
photographs, I tried something new—for me, anyway. I simply opened the
door to my subject's cages and snapped away, trying hard not to get any litter
boxes, cage bars, or metal walls in the shot. I used my zoom lens, which
meant I could move in for close-ups, and I also had a piece of white foam
board, which I could slip into the larger cages as a background.

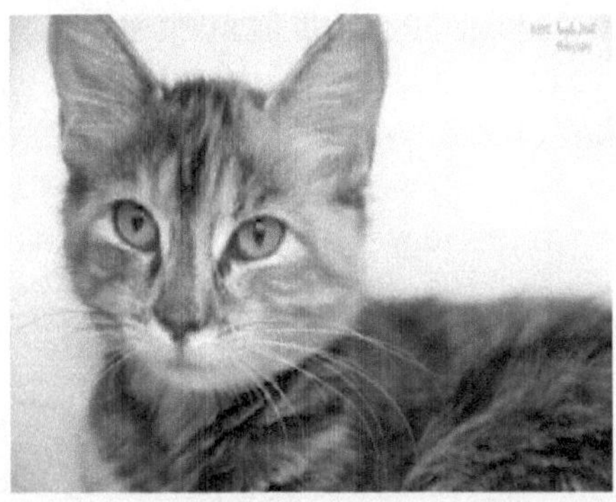

The above photo of Camber was taken in her cage using the piece of white
foam board for a backdrop.

Another time I was told that several of the cats were suffering from
highly contagious respiratory diseases, so we weren't allowed to remove
them from their cages. So if I was going to take pictures at all, I'd have to
take in-the-cage shots. One of the volunteers pointed out that this method had
its advantages—first, the cats weren't as stressed as they were when we
moved them to a new location, and second, I didn't have to worry about
sanitizing fabrics the cat had walked on or curled up in. The white foam
board went in back, so the animal never had a chance to breathe on it or walk
on it, and I zipped it out of the cage the instant after I took the shot.

I wasn't sure this "in the cage" method would result in decent pictures,
but I was pleasantly surprised. Shooting in the cage has become my back-up
method, and one friend who saw my photos from that day remarked that the

cats looked a lot more relaxed than the cats in my previous photos. Of course they did—half of them were still sleepy when I interrupted their afternoon naps!

I did run into one hitch—my standard size white foam board was too large to fit into the smaller cages. So I measured the inner walls of the cages and went home to cut a piece of foam board in half, which allowed me to have two boards, both of which would easily fit into a single cat's cage.

Then I thought about how it'd be nice to have some pretty papers—and what better place to find pretty paper than in a wallpaper book? I called a local wallpaper store, explained that I was photographing animals at the SPCA shelter in town, and he said he'd be happy to give me two discontinued wallpaper books. When I stopped by to pick up the books, he explained that he and his family had adopted two cats from the shelter, so he was always willing to do what he could to help. I also found old wallpaper books for sale on eBay, but why buy them if you can find a store willing to donate them to your cause?

If you don't have access to wallpaper books, you might consider wrapping paper, left over wall paper, or even pieces of fabric. You could cover the foam boards with just about anything and use them for backdrops in a cat's cage.

Once I had the wallpaper pages, I tried to find the best way to temporarily attach a pretty piece of paper to the foam board. My daughter had the brilliant idea of using Velcro—you can buy it either as round sticky-backed circles or in long strips. We went with the package of long strips, and my daughter spent an afternoon sticking Velcro bits onto the foam boards and several pieces of wallpaper. We chose wallpaper pages that were likely to accent the many colors of cats—black, white, calico, gray, and orange. We tried to use several patterned pages for use with solid color cats, and solid or textured pages for use with patterned or calico cats.

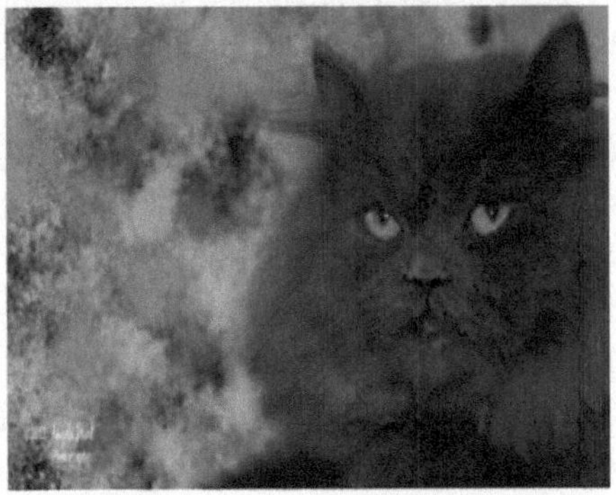

Beautiful Brutus, seen above, didn't even have to budge when we slipped the paper-covered foam board into his cage. (Love that nineties wallpaper!)

Armed with two foam boards and several pages of Velcroed wallpaper, we descended on the cats. I'll be honest—some cats weren't thrilled with me rearranging their bowls and litter boxes so I could slide a patterned "wall" into their abode, but some of them didn't mind at all—they were too busy trying to persuade me to scratch their heads. In any case, the "wallpaper board" is a great idea if your shelter simply doesn't have the space to allow a dedicated room for photography.

Lighting is a major consideration in cat photography, especially if you are shooting indoors under fluorescent bulbs. If you're fortunate, you'll be able to find a small room where you can let the cat roam freely. If there are too many other objects in the room—chairs, filing cabinets, supplies—you may want to remove them, as they will only give the cats something to hide behind.

If you're shooting indoors, of course, you will probably need a flash or other supplemental lighting source. I have noticed that if I use a flash, the cat's eyes are almost narrowed, resulting in a slitty-eyed picture. It is much better to use the room's ambient light or light from a window when photographing indoors. If that fails, try setting the camera's ISO to a higher number. Sometimes a flash or strobe may work, but if you're photographing a cat at close range—such as in his cage—I wouldn't count on getting many good pictures.

If you are thinking of transporting the cats to a studio to be photographed, you may want to think again. Being transported to a strange place—even another room— stresses cats, so your subject may be even less cooperative than cats usually are. Plus, being stressed is not good for a cat's health, especially if it is very young or very old.

Try to understand what the cat has been through: by the time an animal is ready for adoption, he or she has probably already been at the shelter for a week or longer. During that time she has undergone a medical exam, spaying or neutering if the animal wasn't already fixed, and a behavioral evaluation. If the animal had an illness, it may have been held in the medical wing until her treatment was completed. Finally, the cat finds itself in a place with dozens of other meowing cats, trapped in a stainless steel cage with a limited window on the world or a community area with lots of other stranger cats . . . not exactly the happiest of circumstances. No wonder Bootsie, shown below, looks like she'd rather be anywhere than in front of my camera!

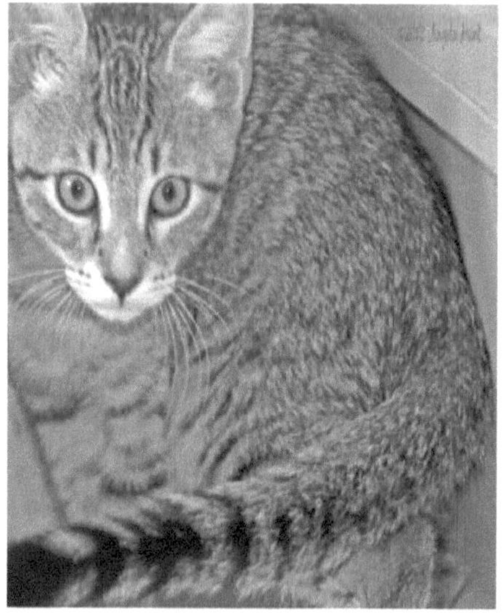

If you are able to find a room for your photography shoot, consider your backdrop. I often use a nine-foot length of white or black craft fur as a backdrop when photographing dogs, but fur isn't going to work with cats— they'll try to climb up the backdrop, and they're likely to topple whatever you're using to hold up your cardboard roll. So you need to go with paper for cats—either paper photography backdrops in white or gray or something of your own choosing. I happened to have a big roll of butcher paper in my garage when I began to photograph cats, so I plan to use it with the cats as soon as we have space available for a more advanced setup. Butcher paper is inexpensive, plus I can rip off the last two feet or so (however much paper the cat walked on) and throw it away before unrolling a new length for my next subject. Streamlined sanitation!

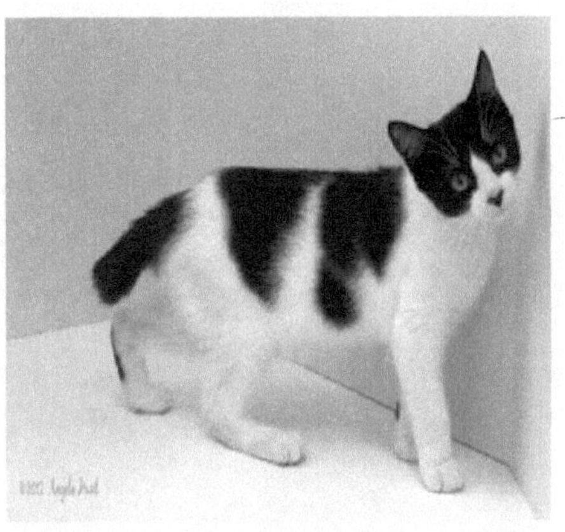

I have also experimented with—and enjoyed—using cardboard project boards as backgrounds. Manny, seen above, is walking on a white poster board and about to rub his head against the corner of a white cardboard project board. Because these project boards (often used for students' science projects) are usually between three and four feet tall, they work very well for cats and small dogs. Their stark white surfaces are smooth and the final look is relatively polished. Some professionals might point out the visible "seam" where the project board meets the poster board flooring, but you could smooth that out in post processing if you wanted to.

When it comes to preparing a place for your shoot, you have several options, but everything will depend upon the facility at your shelter and the space available. But if you come prepared, you can do beautiful "in the cage" photos.

One final note—no matter where you're snapping pictures, if your subject is a lively, frisky cat or kitten, you should probably have someone to assist in case the cat dives out of the cage or off the table. Your hands may be busy with the camera, so someone needs to stand by in case the cat decides to escape. No matter what color they are, know this: capturing kitties is nothing like snapping dogs. A dog can usually be persuaded to sit in front of a backdrop; you'll be lucky if you can entice a cat to do the same. The first time I photographed cats, I spent most of my time chasing the cats with my camera while shouting, "Sit, kitty, sit!" as if I expected them to obey. Ha! Worst of all, I knew I was being ridiculous, but my dog photography habits had become ingrained.

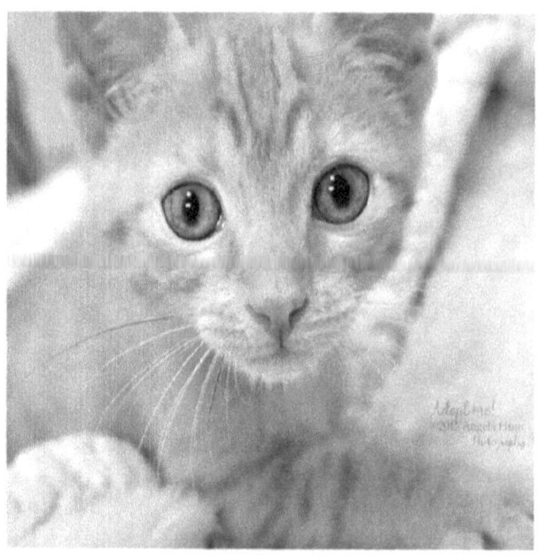

You might be able to get some cats to lie down on a lovely comforter or blanket, but then again, you might not. I did discover that one toy worked well to capture a cat's attention—a stick that had a small, stuffed toy and a bell dangling from the end. By using that to capture the cat's attention, I was able to get the kitty to remain in front of my camera. I was also able to persuade a couple of them to wear ribbons around their necks. But I think I'd be pushing my luck to ask a cat to do much more than that.

In the appendix, you'll find photo galleries from several wonderful photographers who specialize in shelter cats. Let their work inspire you—it certainly has me!

It's a good thing cats are purr-fectly regal just being themselves.

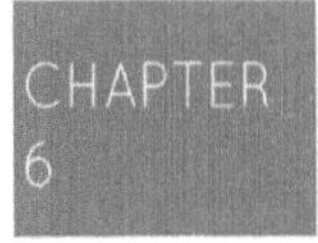

Costumes and Props

Every photographer has his/her own style, and I happen to like portraiture. To me, all dogs are beautiful, so they don't need a lot of extra "stuff" to make them appealing. I try to look for the one thing that will enhance their natural attractiveness and make them look special—a silk ribbon, a scarf, a pearl necklace, or a little bow tie. I am personally not into the "costume" look that sometimes goes as far as to include shoes—I want to enhance the dog, not display a costume.

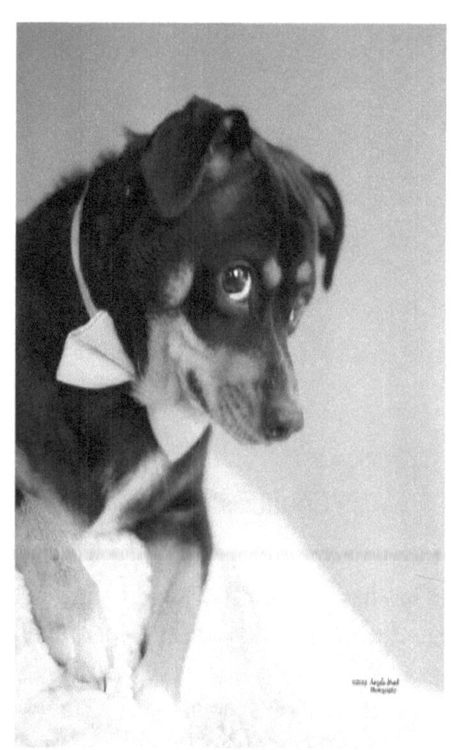

I've tried a lot of things that didn't work so well, and discovered some things that worked in ways I hadn't expected. I learned that stretchy infant headbands work beautifully as soft dog collars. Female dogs look lovely in pearls and beads; male dogs look good in bow ties and knitted scarves. All dogs look good in wide silk ribbons, but don't make the mistake I made and put a beautiful boy in a pink bow!

But whatever you use for the animal's elegant portrait, make sure the prop doesn't overpower the pet. You want the viewer to see the animal's eyes and ears, the elements that reveal a pet's soul and emotions. You want him to look like the beautiful creature he is, not like a dressed-up stuffed animal.

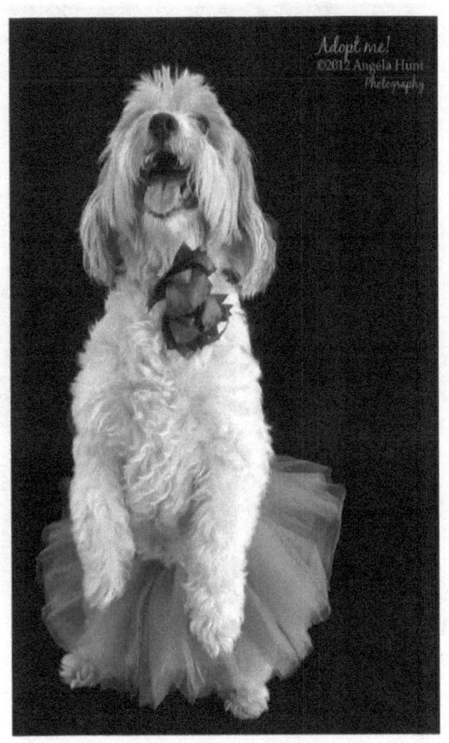

The only time I've used more than one accessory on a dog is when I used something on the animal's "bottom" and wanted something on the "top" to balance out the look. Even then, the second something should be, to my way of thinking, on the small side.

Whatever you choose to adorn the dog or cat, please make sure it complements the dog's breed and personality. I wouldn't put a tutu on a St. Bernard's waistline, and I wouldn't tie a bulky knitted scarf on a dainty Maltese.

And always remember—sometimes the best adornment is nothing at all.

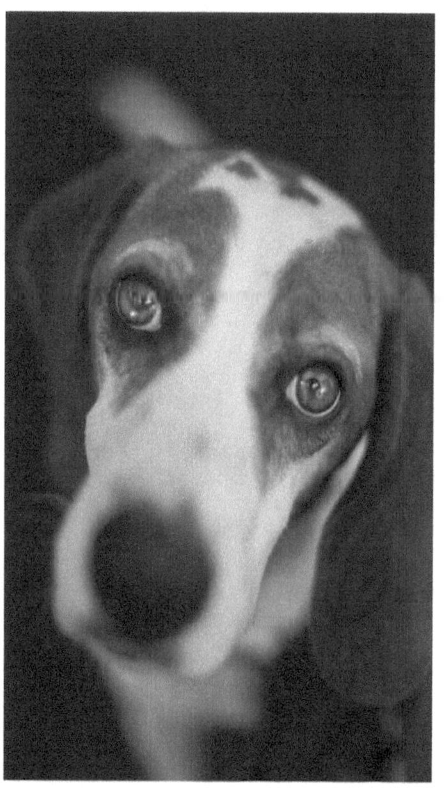

PHOTO

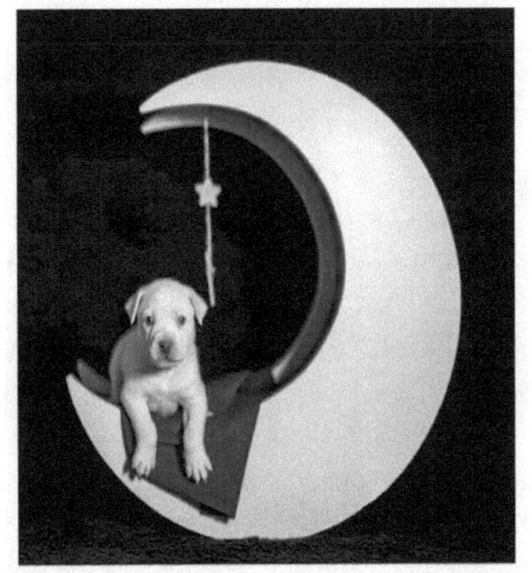

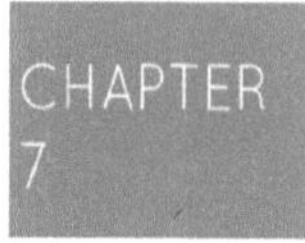

After the Session: Post-Processing

Once I have finished taking pictures, I leave the animal shelter and head home to put in roughly twice as much time as I spent with the animals. I use my card reader or camera cord to transfer the photos from my camera to my computer, and I save them all in a folder simply called "SPCA." Once the photos have transferred, I open the Finder window (I work on a Mac) to look at them. If you're working on a PC, you could use Windows Explorer.

In the Finder window, with the "view" setting set to order the photos according to creation date, I can simply scroll through the photos and look for shots that have potential. If I spot a photo that appears particularly good, I change the name from "DSC1005" to "Spot good smile" or something similar. It's important to place the dog's name first, because that's how I'm going to find that particular photo in this collection when it's time to settle on the final shots for post processing.

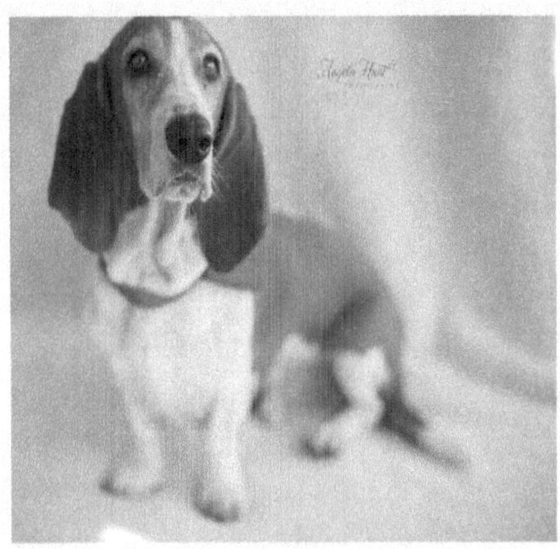

As I skim through the photos, the primary element I'm looking for is something that evokes an emotional response: something that makes me smile, say "awww," or lean forward to take a closer look. For any given dog, I may find three pictures with potential or I may find twenty. But if I've taken lots of photos, I've greatly improved my chances of finding something special.

When I've gone through all the day's images, I close the Finder window and open my photo post processing program. It really doesn't matter what program you use—you may want to use something heavy duty (and expensive!) like Photoshop, or you may prefer something simple that came with your computer. As long as the program will allow you to crop photos and save images in different resolutions, you should be fine. Obviously, the more complicated the program, the more options you will have.

In the beginning, I used Photoshop Elements, which is quite powerful but not nearly as expensive or complicated as the full version of Photoshop. Unless you plan on working with lots of graphic design, Photoshop Elements may have every capability you need.

Once I've gone through all the photos, I open Photoshop Elements and click to arrange the files in my "SPCA" folder in alphabetical order—that way, all the photos with a particular dog's name will be grouped together. When I open the files that begin with "Spot," they all appear in my post processing program's "tray."

By the way, while many professional photographers shoot in RAW, meaning that the camera does absolutely no processing before the photos are transferred; most hobbyists shoot in the JPEG format. The image will be compressed, but I doubt you'd notice the difference in quality with the naked eye. I've used both, and the one thing I like about shooting in RAW is that I can batch process the files. They will not automatically open in Photoshop Elements, but will instead open in an Adobe program for RAW files. In this program, I can adjust the lighting and exposure of all the photos in one action, saving time. Once I've adjusted all that day's photos, I open all of them in Photoshop Elements to do the detail work.

(By the way, why is our after-the-shoot work called *post* processing? Because a digital camera *processes* the photo when it turns what it sees into the pixels of a file. We're going to take it a step beyond that.)

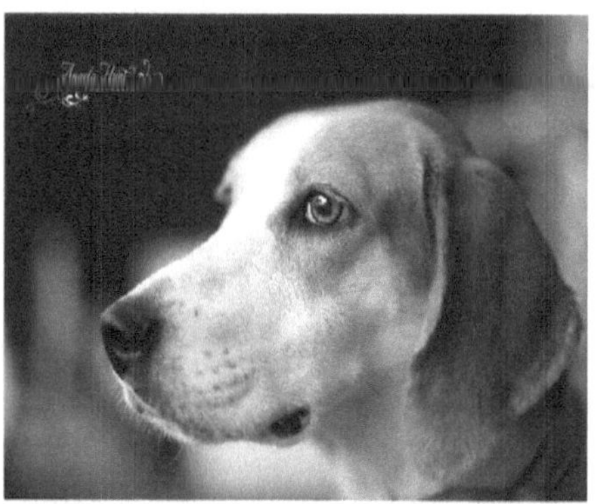

When all of my photos-with-potential are open in my post processing program, I begin the job of whittling them down to three. Several shots will be similar—for instance, I might have four shots of Spot sitting and facing left. I compare the first one to the second one, and delete the weakest. Then I compare the surviving photo to the next, and delete the weakest of the pair. Sometimes the photos may appear to be identical; if so, I simply delete one. I keep working, comparing and contrasting, until I have narrowed the selection down to three.

Now comes the fun part. Some photos might have a noisy background, a leash, or a human hand in the picture—this will either have to be cropped out or cloned out with a technique in Photoshop Elements. Obviously, the fewer distractions in the photo, the easier the post processing will be.

    You can post process your photos any way you like, but here are the steps I usually take.

    1. Photoshop Elements has an automatic adjust; I click the button and see what happens. It usually corrects color tones and white balance, but if I don't like the result, I undo whatever the automatic button did.

    2. Next, I crop the photo so that the subject fills two-thirds of the picture. The only time I would keep a subject in the dead center is if I had no choice or if the subject was in the center of matching objects—a dog sitting between two identical pillars. In that case, it'd be natural for him to be in the center.

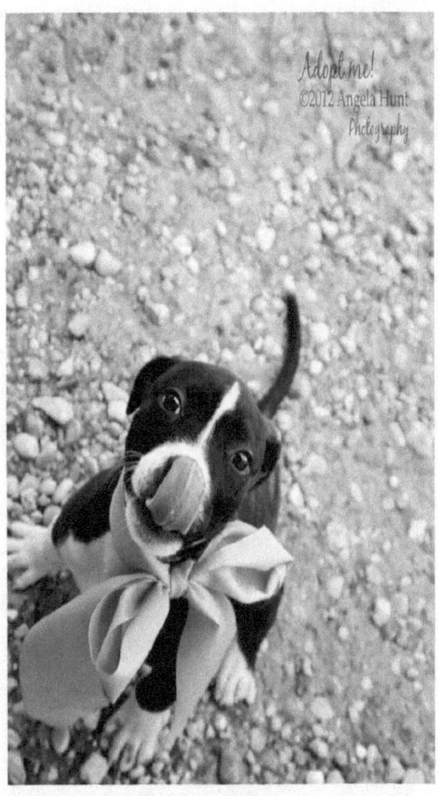

When cropping, don't forget that "white space" or "negative space" can be a way to emphasize your subject. Don't feel that you have to crop the photo right up against the subject's body. Leave some room for the viewer to breathe. In this photo of Dipstick, for instance, though I could have cropped it closer to the puppy's body, I left the empty space because it emphasizes his small size.

3. After cropping, I get rid of any noticeable collars, leashes, spots on blankets, or anything else that distracts from the photo. If the dog has the large shaved square on his hindquarters that comes along with heart worm treatment, I fill that in with fur—not to deceive anyone, but to give an impression of what he will look like once the fur has grown back. You can remove objects through several different post processing tools such as clone painting or applying layers. If the object isn't distracting, I leave it alone.

If a dog has a condition or deformity that isn't going away, I leave it. To remove it, I think, is a form of false advertising. Besides, sometimes it's our weaknesses that make us the most unusual and unique.

4. An important step—check for eye goobers. Use one of your post processing program's tools to paint out or remove those distracting marks and/or smears around the dog's eyes. A viewer's gaze will be naturally drawn to that area, and sometimes you have to really zoom in to see white specks or discolorations around the eye, nose, or mouth.

Along with checking for eye gunk, check the subject's eye color. Humans often get "red eye" from flash photography; dogs and cats may get a case of green or gray eye. If so, you can repair the condition easily.

In the following photo of Ruby, you can clearly see gray/greenish eyes from the flash. In the second photo, taken in the same session, the "green eye" has been darkened to a more natural shade.

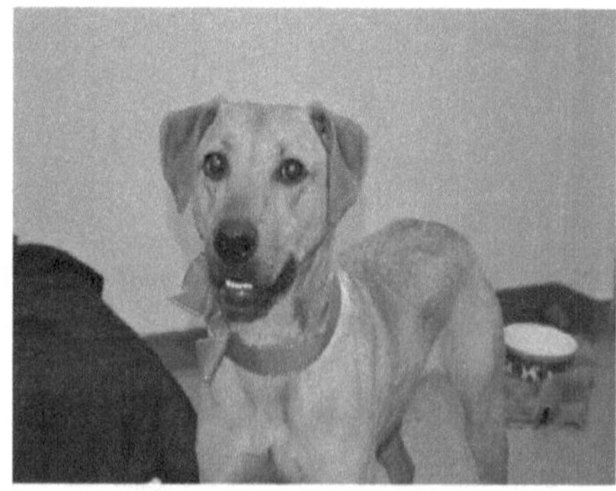

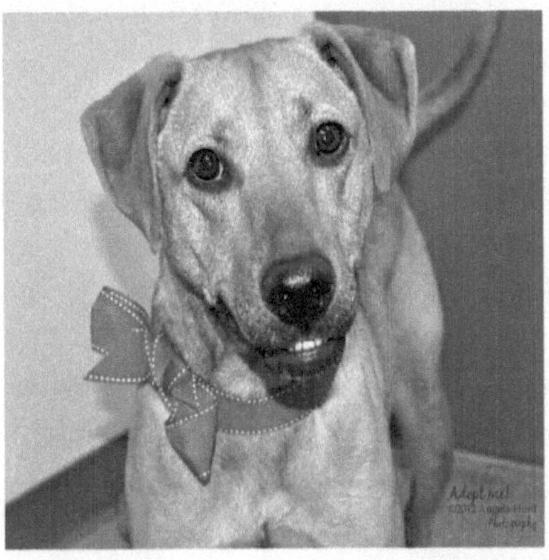

The ghostly eye is easy to eradicate in your post processing program. To remove it, look for a tool that can darken objects—in Photoshop and Photoshop Elements, it's the "burn" tool. Simply set the tool—which looks like a circle—over the green glow and click until the ghostly shade disappears. Be careful, however—you want *some* light to remain in the eye. Without it the eyes look dead, as in the following photo of Baby, where I applied the burn tool with too heavy a hand. You don't want to create a "zombie eye" effect. Not even pearls can help pull that off.

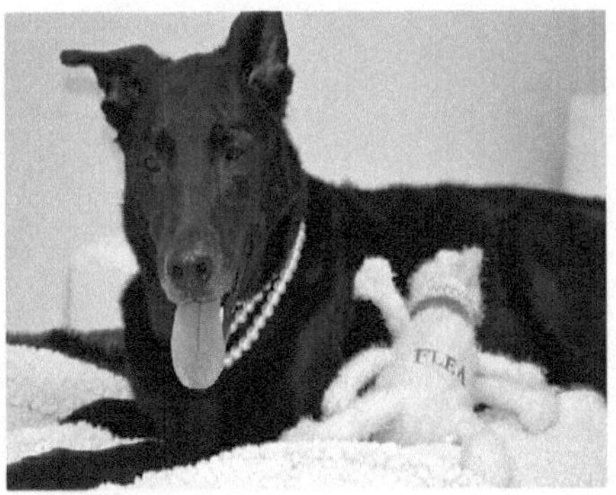

5. Next, adjust the color. Sometimes you can make the color more saturated and enliven a photo. Again, these tools will vary according to what program

you're using, but go ahead and make the color pop if you want to. Just don't do anything so drastic that the animal no longer looks like the same creature.

Your post processing program may have all kinds of filters and effects you can apply to photos—experiment with them if you like, but apply them with caution. If you get too artsy (and it's easy to be tempted), your animal shelter may find the photos unusable. Often shelters send photos to local newspapers for weekly rescue features, and fancy effects don't always translate into newsprint.

But if you want to experiment, search the Internet for "free actions." Lots of companies make these available to photographers, and you apply them like an effect within Photoshop Elements. You can find actions that affect color, size, luminosity, and even apply watermarks.

6. Finally, apply your watermark/copyright notice. Anyone who creates an artistic work—be it book, article, photograph, or song—has the right to be acknowledged as the creator of that work. You also have the right to be credited with that work, so you have the right to put © 2013 John Doe somewhere on your photograph. It's not required, but if you're happy with your work, why not sign it?

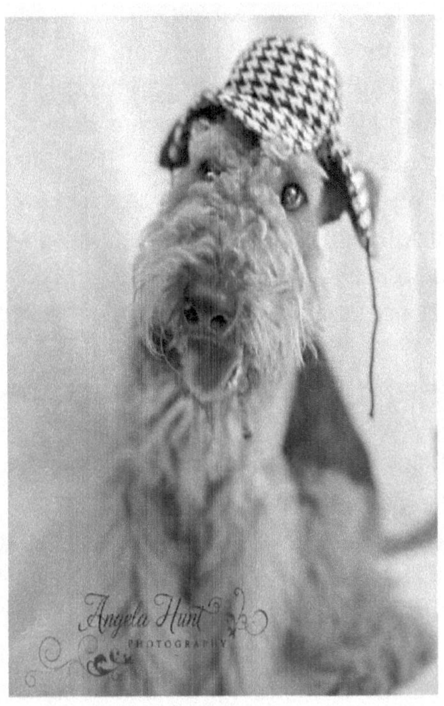

Many people are confused by copyright, but the law is really simple. A creative work—no matter what it is—is copyrighted the moment you create it. Applying the copyright notice only reminds the public that you are the creator. You do not have to submit any paperwork to the national copyright office in order to register your copyright, though you are certainly free to do so. That step is optional.

By the way, beware of entering any photo contest that states, usually in fine print, that by entering the contest you are transferring your copyright to XYC Company. If you enter anyway, the sponsoring company will own the copyright and will be able to use your photo wherever they want to use it—without your permission and without offering you any compensation.

But I don't care about copyright, you may be thinking. *Why do I need to understand it if I'm planning on donating my efforts to a charitable organization?*

You need to know about copyright because I've read enough posts on photography discussion boards to know that misinformation is rampant, even among those who work at well-known organizations. And you never know when you might want to submit one of your photos for a calendar, a newsletter, or even post it to your blog or Facebook. If you didn't own the copyright, you wouldn't have the right to do any of those things.

If you are an employee of the animal shelter—if you earn a paycheck from them in your role as a photographer—then your photos would be covered under "**work for hire**" and the copyright would belong to your employer, the animal shelter. If you are a volunteer, however, and do not earn a paycheck from the organization, then the copyright to your photos belongs to you.

When I began working at my local shelter, I signed an agreement giving the shelter the right to use my photographs however they would like to use them. They do not have to pay me a penny; I am freely giving them the right to use my work to aid their cause. (Incidentally, they do *not* have the right to use my work in any derogatory way; to do so would violate the moral rights clause of copyright law). But even though I have given permission for them to use my photos, they do not own the copyright to those photos. Yes, they may have custody of the dogs I photograph. Yes, they may provide a place for me to take the photos. But I provide my equipment, my time, and my expertise, such as it is, so our exchange could be called a trade.

If you'd like more information on copyright law as it pertains to photography, visit http://www.photosecrets.com/copyright

7. The last step in my post processing procedure is to save and distribute the photos. Your shelter will probably have their own preferences, but my local shelter wants us to submit two copies of each of the three photos per animal: one copy in high resolution (300 dpi) and one copy for publication on the web (72 dpi). The 72 dots-per-inch photos are smaller and easier for people to download from the web while the high res photos are often used in posters, bulletins, brochures, newsletters, and other printed materials. The printed quality of a 300 dpi photo is much better than that of a 72 dpi shot.

(And, incidentally, you should post low resolution copies of your photos on sites such as Facebook, Blogger, etc. People will be able to *see* them, but any attempt to *print* them will end in a pixelated photo. Not good.)

For more information on post processing digital photos, check this website: http://photo.net/learn/digital-post-processing/ .

8. One final note: when you take photos of shelter animals, please upload them as soon as you can. Animals can move in and out of the shelter with

very little notice, and you want your subject to have his best chance at being adopted. So please do your post processing and uploading as soon as possible so your precious cat or dog can present his best face to the world. You will never know what a difference your photo *could* have made unless you post it.

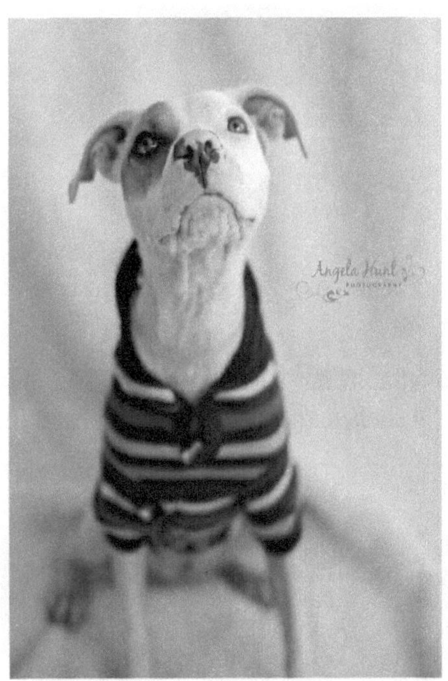

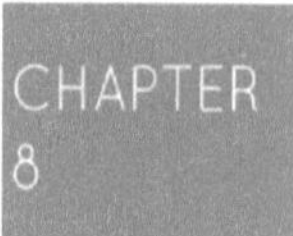

Shelter Photography Do's and Don'ts

Like anything, photography has a learning curve, so I'm happy to share some of my less-than-ideal shots in the hope that you'll learn from my mistakes.

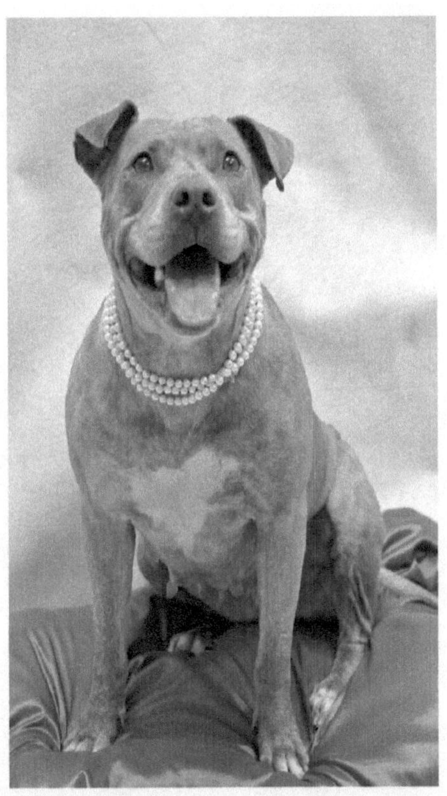

Beautiful Elsa: Better to have the dog looking at the top of your head (and at the viewer) . . .

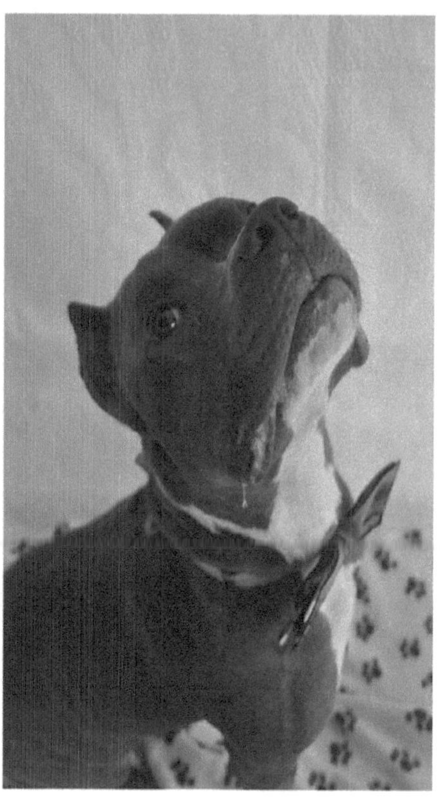

. . . than lifting his head so high that he seems to cut himself off from everyone (this image ended up in the trash folder). By the way, this backdrop is a shower curtain I found in a T.J. Maxx clearance bin. Shower curtains make great backdrops, and you can hang them onto a chain link fence with shower hooks.

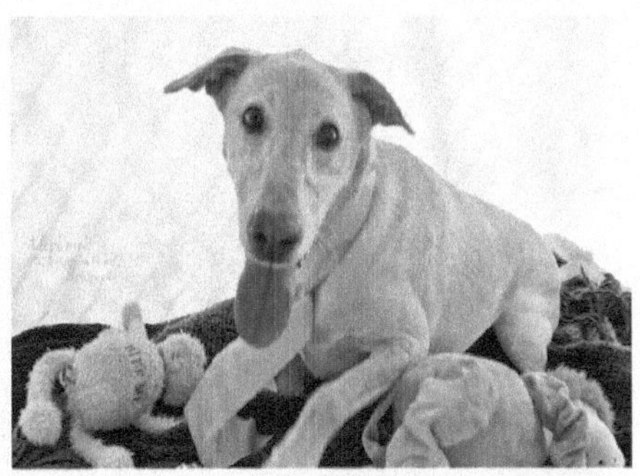

Copper is a beautiful boy (who loves toys!), but that see-through felt
backdrop had to go. It worked well indoors (in Elsa's picture, for instance),
but not when the sun was shining through it.

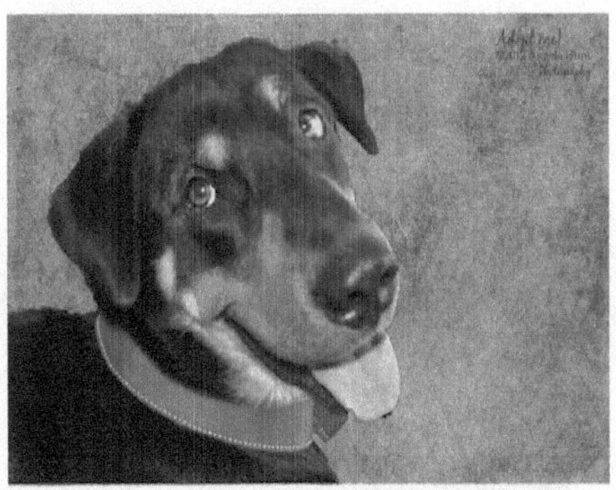

If I had to do Copper's photo over, I'd cut out that white backdrop and insert
a background layer from Photoshop Elements, as I did in this picture of
Benji, who simply didn't want to sit in my prepared area and chose to sit next
to an unattractive chain link fence.

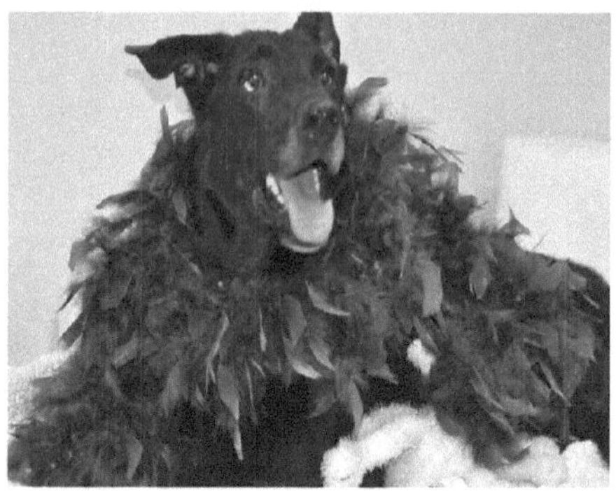

This photo of Baby, one of the first pictures I took at the shelter, caused me to set a new rule for myself: *Props are good, but they should accent the dog and never overpower her.* Baby was a good sport, though. Didn't eat a single feather.

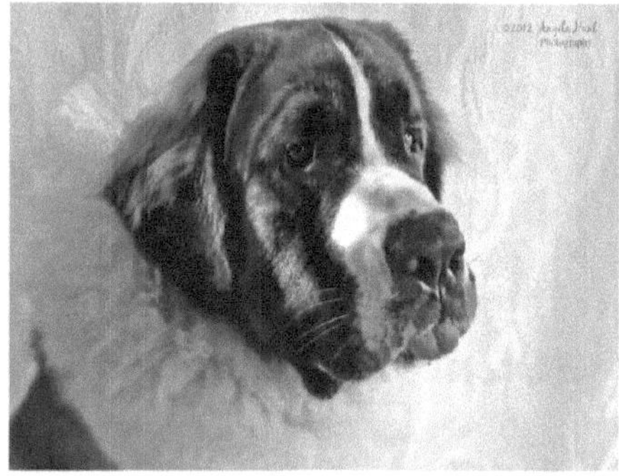

This headshot of beautiful St. Bernard Mac in his ruff works much better than Baby in that long feather boa. (Hint: baby tutus make great neck ruffs for big dogs!)

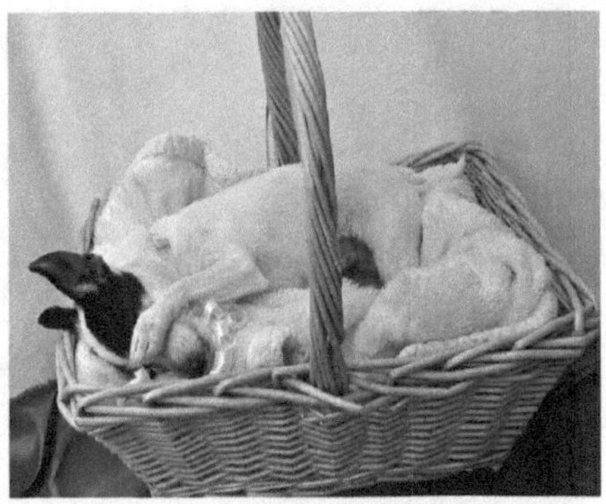

Zelda struck an adorable pose in my basket, but the effect would have been so much better if I'd lined the basket with a contrasting color and used something other than a white ribbon around her neck. As it is, you can hardly tell where the dog ends and the blanket begins!

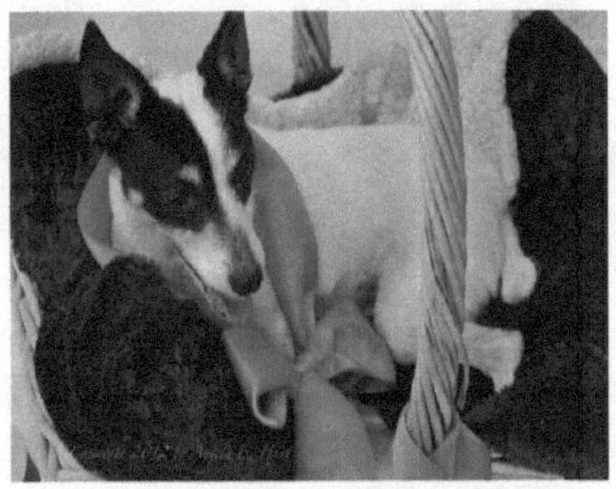

I later reshot Zelda's picture with a pink bow and a brown blanket in the basket. Much better—but she wouldn't cover her eyes for me. Sigh.

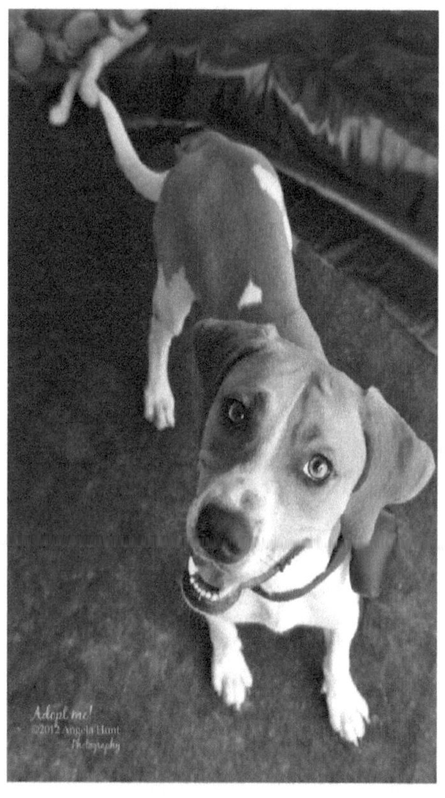

If a dog will not sit and pose on your shiny piece of brown satin, take his picture from above—and let all those luxurious fabrics contrast nicely against his coat. Hint: I shop in the remnant bin at fabric stores. You can find one- and two-yard remnants of really pretty solid fabrics for half of what they would have cost on the bolt. Just make sure they're machine washable. (Ditto for any satin bows you plan to tie around a dog's neck.)

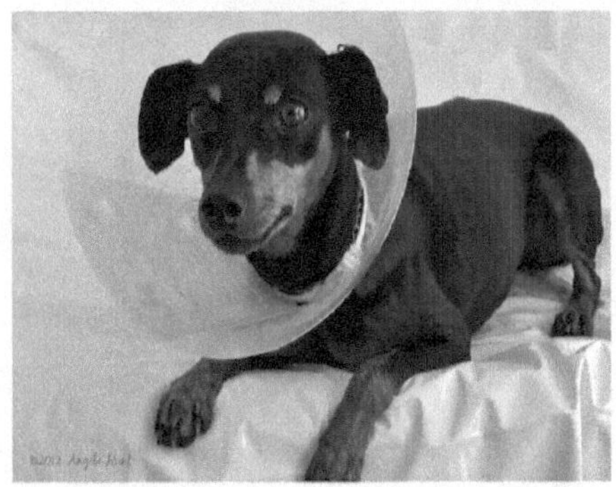

If a dog is wearing a protective cone for some reason (Cash was worrying at the sutures from his neutering operation), you don't want to emphasize it. So choose backdrop and blanket colors to match the cone, not draw attention to it. I was fortunate enough to find a piece of white shiny pleather in a remnant bin.

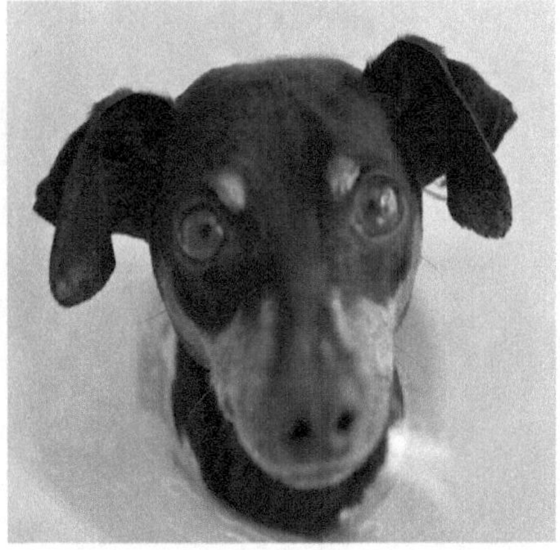

Or you could move in for such a close up that the cone isn't even visible. What *is* important? The dog's eyes and ears.

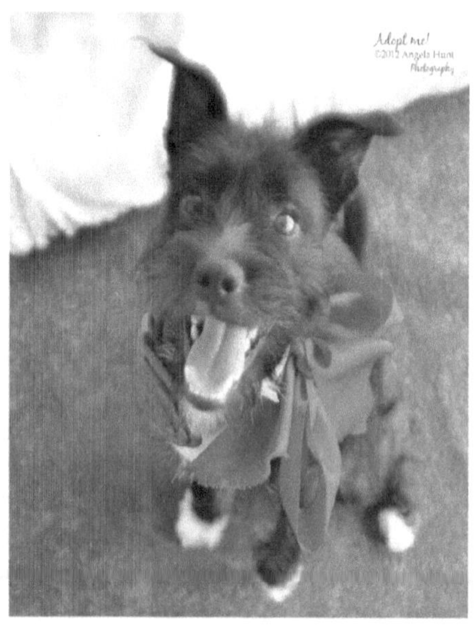

Too much adornment is simply too much. Cindy's bow was actually part of the ribbon supporting the rose, but when they both appeared in the shot, the result was overkill.

Much better to have only the one red rose visible (as below). The toy? Because it's a different color, I don't think it competes with the rose or the dog. And the fact that it's a toy (one she was actually playing with as I snapped the photo) reveals that Cindy is playful.

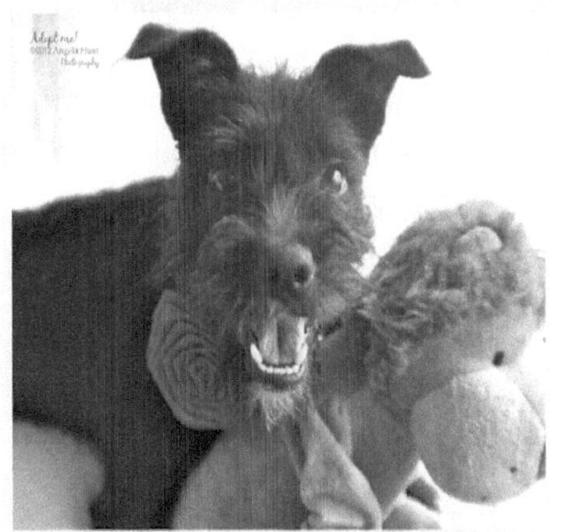
Adopt me!
©2012 Angela Hunt
Photography

Close-ups are beautiful, providing that the camera focus on the dog's eyes and not his nose. The eyes reveal the spirit within the animal.

Alice lost a baby tooth while she was chewing on this tennis ball, so I had "clone out" some of the blood on the ball. I didn't want people to think she was a man-eater in the making.

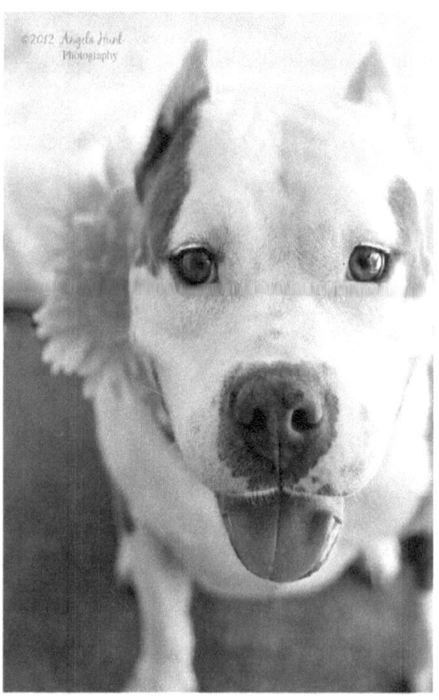

A close up of our beautiful Rain. Close-ups are a great way to feature depth of field—the blurry background which serves to accent the foreground and Rain's sweet face. Greater depth of field is the result of choosing a larger (lower number) aperture.

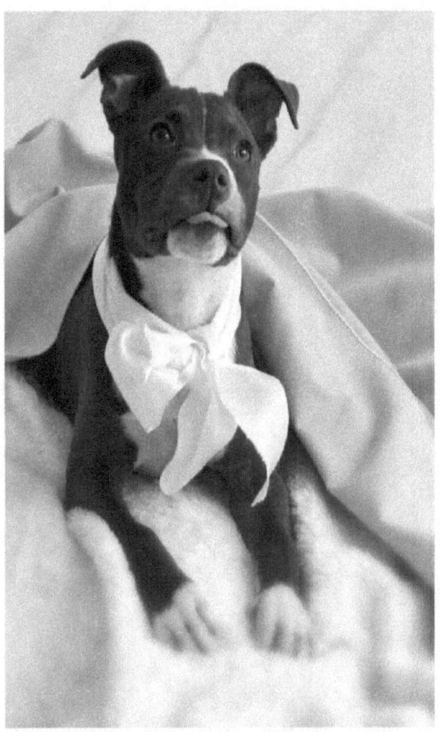

Some photos are the result of serendipity. I had the orange linen tablecloth hung over the white felt backdrop, but a gust of wind blew it down and onto the puppy. Fortunately, Lady took it in stride and I got an adorable picture!

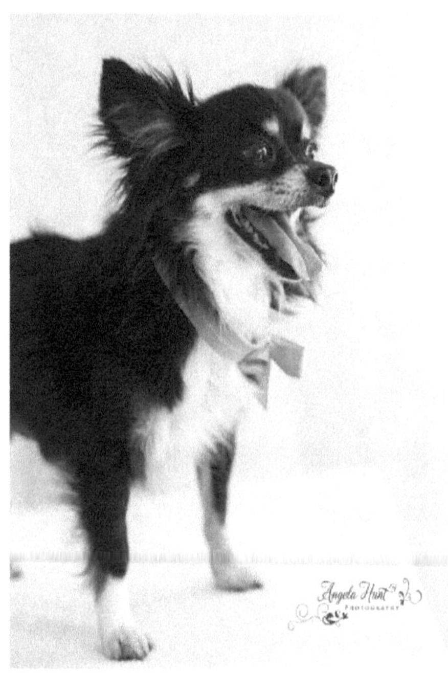

Be careful when you crop, whether in camera or out—I cropped this picture in a hurry and without thinking, but the moment it posted online, I realized that I had made this poor dog look like he only had two legs. Oops. The image would have been salvageable if I had cropped it for a head and shoulders shot or left more of his back leg in the frame.

By the way, if your camera gives you a choice, shoot in the "large" picture mode—that will give you more room to crop without losing quality in your photos. Yes, the photos will take up more room on your camera or memory card, so buy a card with plenty of storage space.

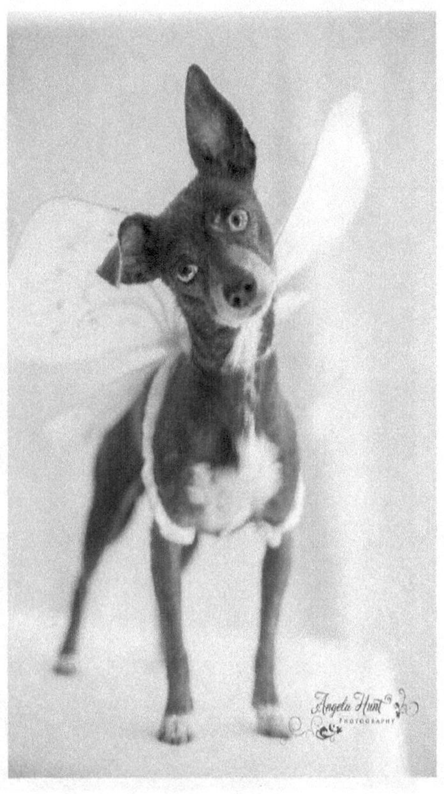

Ah, the head tilt. I don't think any pose is more endearing, so when I get that tilted head—"Aw, come on, can I?"—I can't resist. The best thing about it that I have learned how to get a head tilt on command—well, my technique is about 80 percent effective. The secret? Take a few pictures, then introduce a strange sound into the conversation. Odds are you'll get that endearing quizzical look.

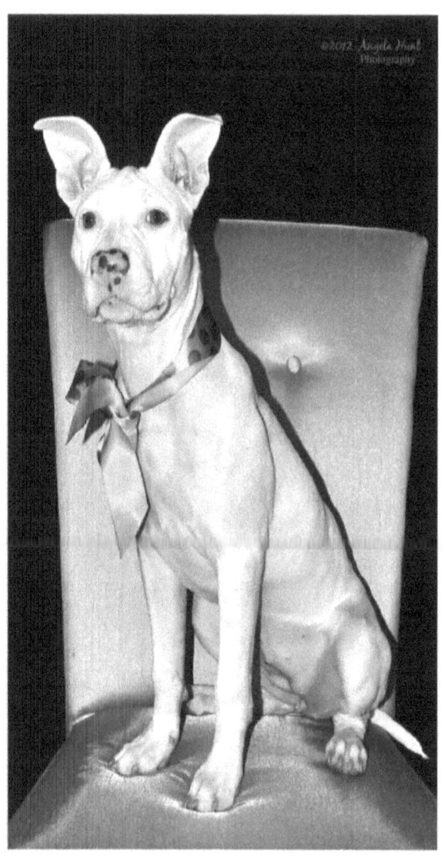

I bought three yards of a black craft fur at the fabric store to use for white or light-colored dogs. When post processing, I darken the blacks until I can't see the difference between the "floor" and the back wall. This completely highlights the dogs and yields a professional seamless look.

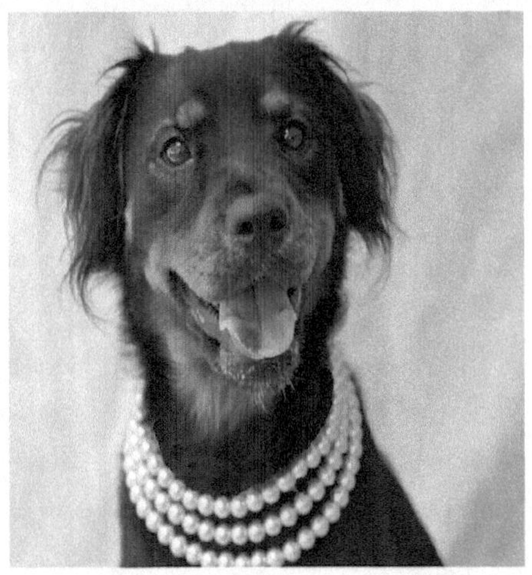

Some photos simply make me laugh, like this picture of Nana. Cropped the way it is, she looks so human! Maybe it's the Barbara Bush pearls. Hint: Check thrift stores for simple, cheap costume jewelry.

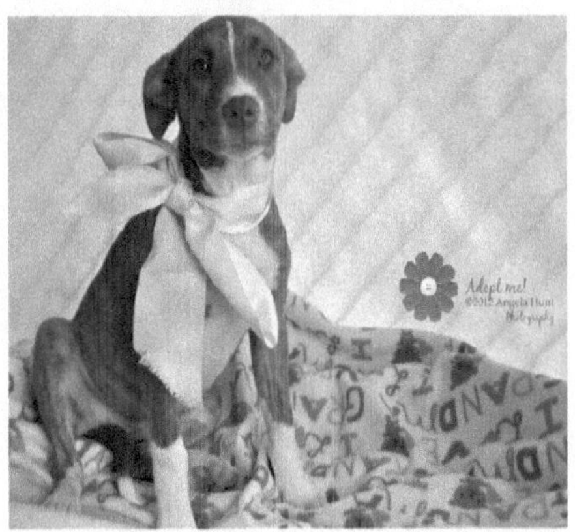

A note about graphics, like the flower in the picture above: I think graphics are like props—fine, as along as they're simple and appropriate and unobtrusive—but my shelter asks that photographers confine graphics to the 72 resolution photos we contribute for the web. We also donate high res photos at 300 dpi, and we keep those free from graphics because we don't know how the shelter will use them—photos, posters, newspaper ads, etc. Check with your shelter and see how they feel about graphics, the size of watermarks, etc.

One more thing: you'll undoubtedly get lots of different and unexpected shots when you're shooting in burst mode. Just be sure that your photo doesn't show too many teeth, as in the photo below. This girl was really a sweetheart, but this photo, snapped in mid-yawn, made her look more like a ferocious monster.

For the same reason, I try to avoid photos that show the dog ripping into a stuffed animal or chewing on my camera bag. I don't want a prospective adopter to see that image and imagine that the dog will do the same thing to their sofa cushions. I can't guarantee that the dog will have perfect manners, but training is part of responsible dog ownership, isn't it?

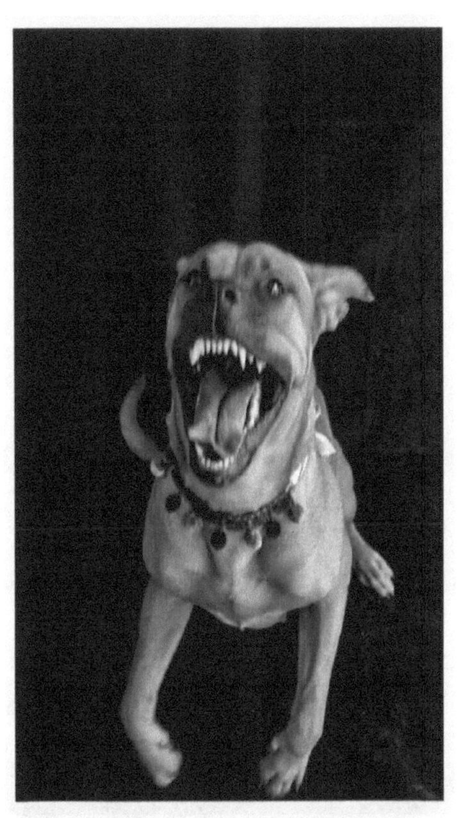

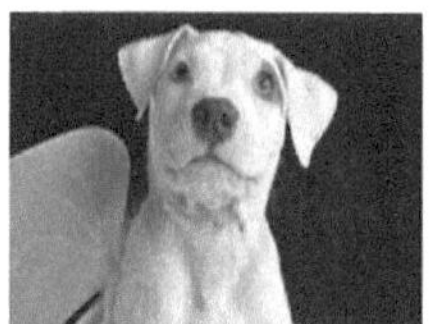

A WALK THROUGH DIGITAL POST-PROCESSING

WE BEGIN with a photo of adorable Jue, a pit bull puppy (whom I would have adopted in a heartbeat!). Jue is wearing angel wings, but they're crooked in this picture, so they look a bit odd. Jue also has some little scratches on her chest and above her left eye from tussling with her sister.

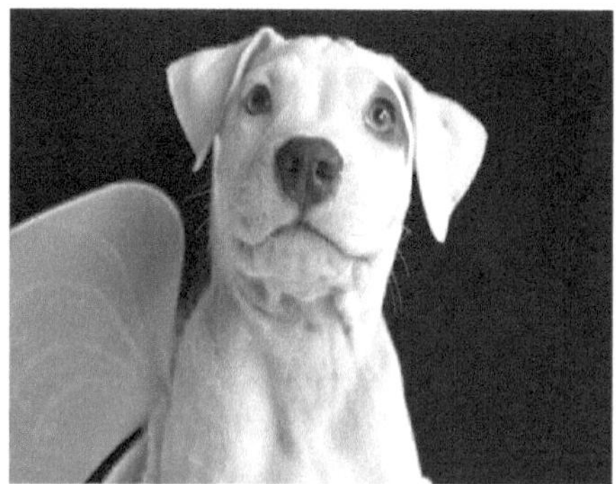

The first step, seen above, was to automatically correct the levels and contrast. As you can see, the effect is not much different, but that's reassuring. The contrast was good coming out of the camera.

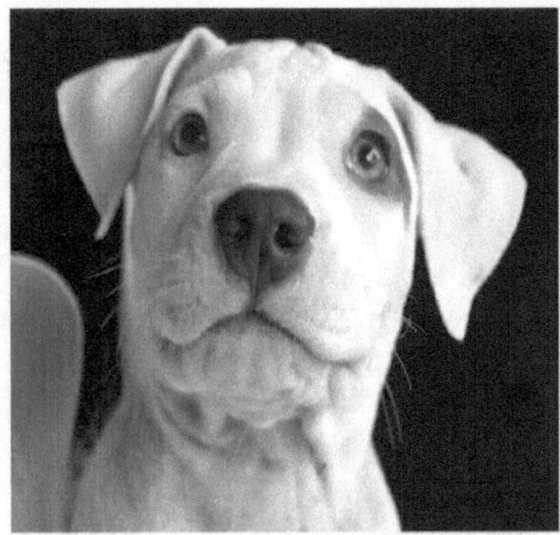

The second step, above, was to crop the picture so the puppy fills two-thirds of the frame. I'm going to get rid of that awkward single wing, so the picture will be better balanced without it. I have also shortened what appeared to be a very long neck. Notice that a good crop brings the puppy closer to the viewer.

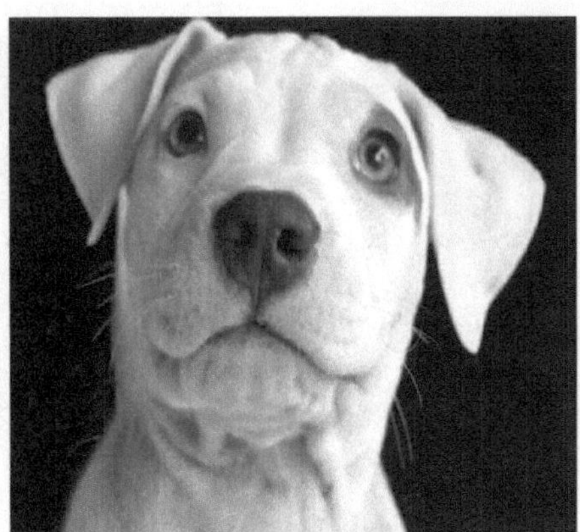

The next step was to use the clone tool to "black out" the unbalanced and unwanted wing. To clone, I "selected" an area containing the color I wanted (black), then I moved my cursor over the area I didn't want, thus "painting out" the unwanted pixels.

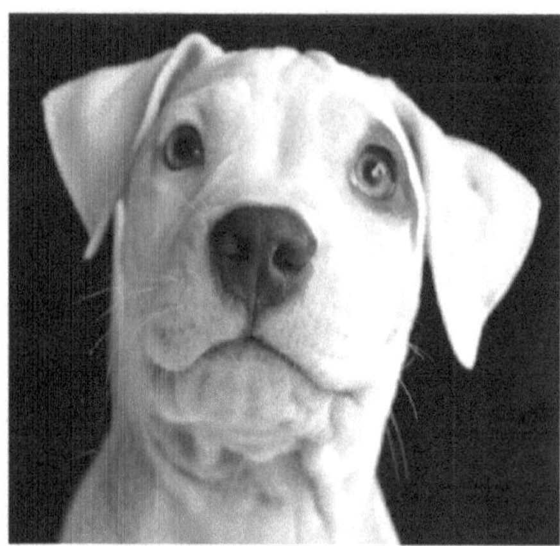

In the next step, I used the "healing brush" in Photoshop Elements to take out the scratch above Jue's left eye and the scratch on the deepest fold at her neck. I didn't alter the permanent appearance of the dog, I simply touched up her photo.

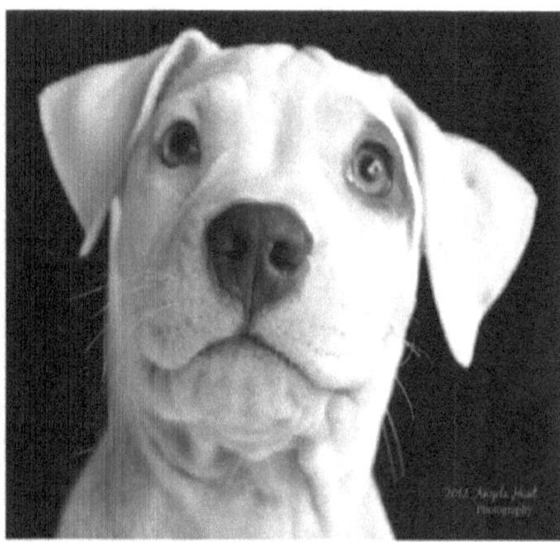

In the last step, I simply added my copyright/watermark in the lower right corner. All I have to do now is save the photos in a format for sharing with the animal shelter and then upload them to our transfer site.

An extra technique worth your time—and one I didn't know about when I worked on the photo of Jue.

Enhancing the eye shine.

Why does eye shine make such a difference? Because eyes are the window to the soul, in people and in pets. The wide eyes of a dog can speak to the viewer's heart, so the more appealing we can make those eyes, the more effective the picture will be.

Example: Twiggy—below—without and with enhanced eye shine. The effect will vary with each picture, of course, but I think you'll agree that she seems more "present" in the second image.

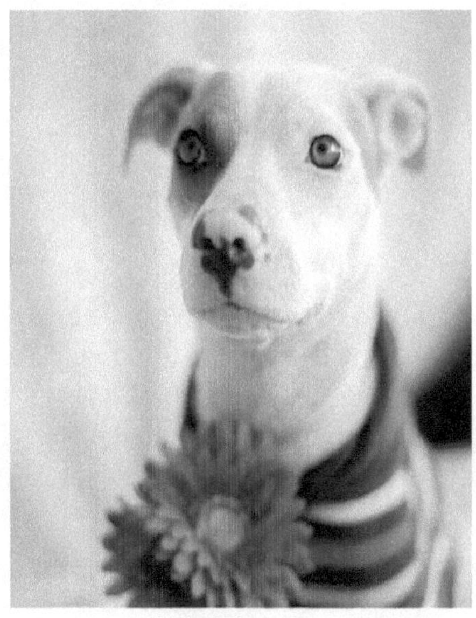

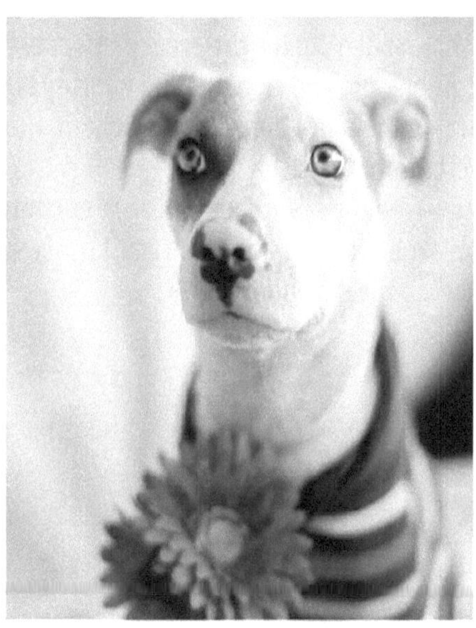

So how do you do it? There's an easy way and a better way.

The *easy* way is simply to take the dodge tool in Photoshop or Photoshop Elements (it looks like a ping pong paddle) and run it over the dog's eyes, especially over any catchlights in the eye. Avoid running it over the pupil, as it tends to make dark colors look cloudy. You should see it lighten the pixels beneath it.

The *better* way requires you to work with layers in Photoshop Elements or Photoshop. Don't panic—this one's easy.

First, simultaneously hit the command key and the J key to copy the background layer you're working on. Then, with the new copy layer selected and highlighted, look up to the top left of the layer panel to find the blending modes option. It will be set to "normal" by default, so scroll down until it says "screen." Clicking this will make the copy layer super-bright.

Now, simultaneously press the option or alt key with the "add layer mask" icon in the layers panel—it looks like a shaded rectangle with a circle in it. This should place a black layer mask over your picture, restoring it to its original color.

What it has actually done is put a black layer over that super-bright screen. Now you're going to select the brush over in the tools panel, and reduce or enlarge it (using the right and left bracket keys) until you can fit it inside the dog's eye. After making certain that you have BLACK as the foreground color in your tools panel, carefully run the brush around the iris of the subject's eye, making sure to also paint over the catchlights. This will remove that black layer and expose the super-bright pixels underneath. If you paint too much, click on the arrows on your color tools, reversing the black and white, and paint with white. (Remember: white conceals, black reveals).

Now look at your photo. If the effect is too strong, simply lower the opacity of that layer a bit using the slider in the layers panel. You don't want to have the animal looking like a vampire dog, but keep in mind that a web photo will be resized. The effect will be greatly diminished when the photo has been made smaller.

This technique is especially effective on dogs whose eyes are partially hidden by hair or swallowed up by black fur. If you have a picture without any catchlights at all, you should paint some in.

To do that, I use the smudge tool (it looks like an index finger pointing downward), and make sure that white is my foreground color. With the smudge tool activated, make sure to select a wide brush and then check the "finger painting" box in the smudge tool controls. Then very lightly and quickly "paint" a small stroke of white in each eye. Zoom in to do this, then zoom out to check the effect. It should help your subject look much more alert and alive.

And that's how we want him to look, isn't it?

Ten Commandments of Rescue Animal Photography

1. Do be calm and confident with the animals. Your attitude will transfer to them.

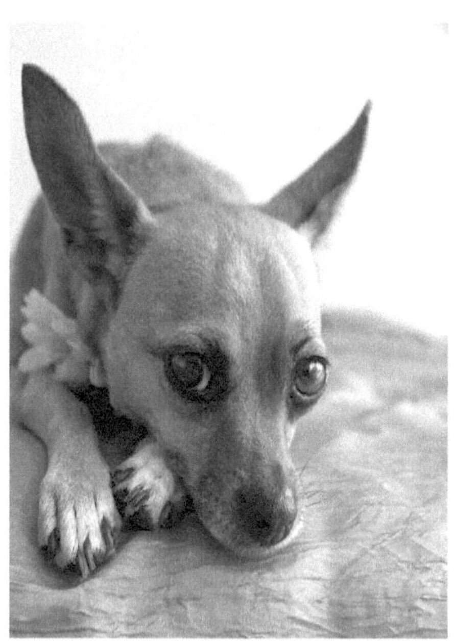

2. Do be willing to make strange noises, wave toys, and get down on the floor. Leave your dignity at home, and don't take every shot from a standing position.

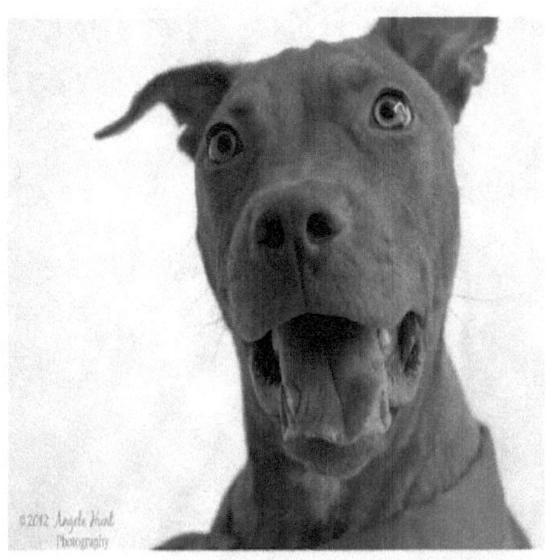

3. Do get on your subject's eye level. Eye-to-eye connection is powerful.

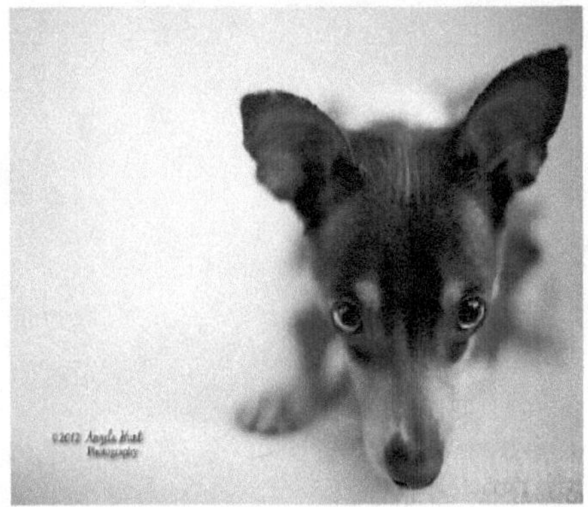

4. Do opt for plain, noncompeting backgrounds whenever possible.

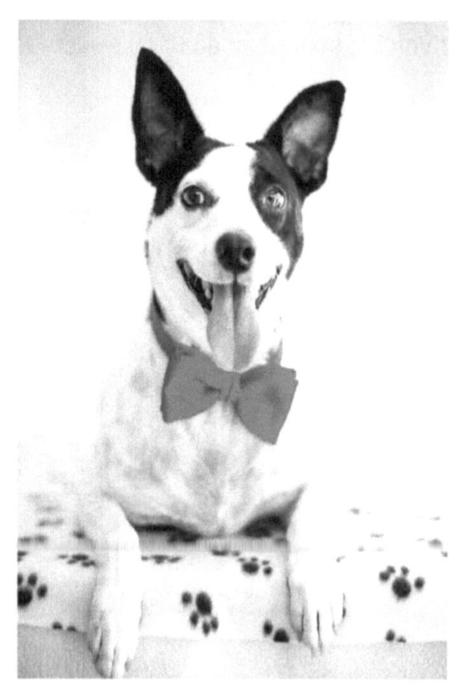

5. Do try to fill the frame with the animal, not his surroundings.

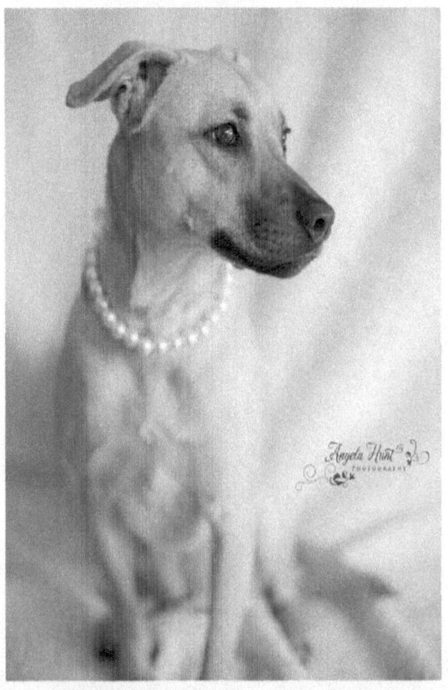

6. Do be willing to try different angles. Why not take a shot of Buster's feet, Becca's nose, or Jack's tail? But don't forget the eyes. They speak a wordless language everyone understands.

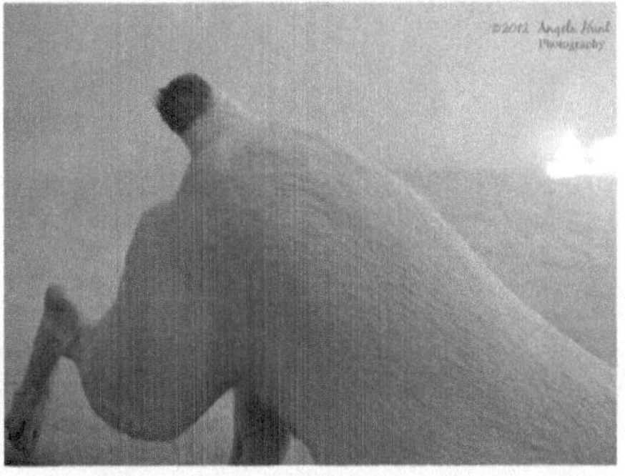

7. Do be patient. Some animals need time to settle down and play.

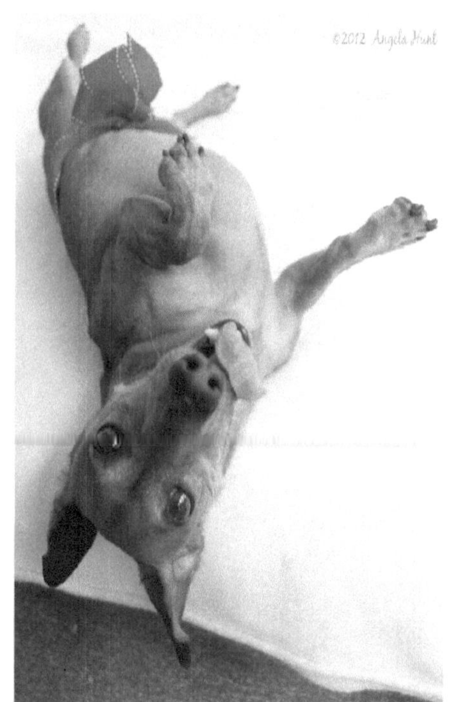

8. If you're photographing a dog, do take him for a short walk before the shoot. Don't tire him out or get him overheated, but do get to know him a bit before you start asking him to pose.

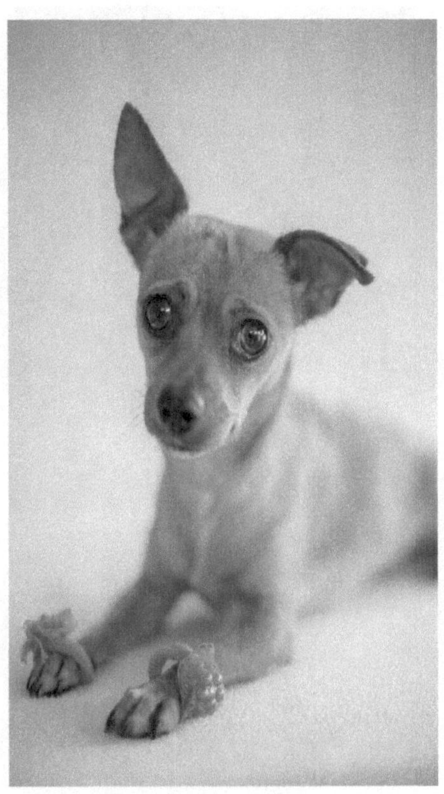

9. Do try a few props, but don't let them overpower your subject. If the adornment is the first thing someone notices, it's probably too much.

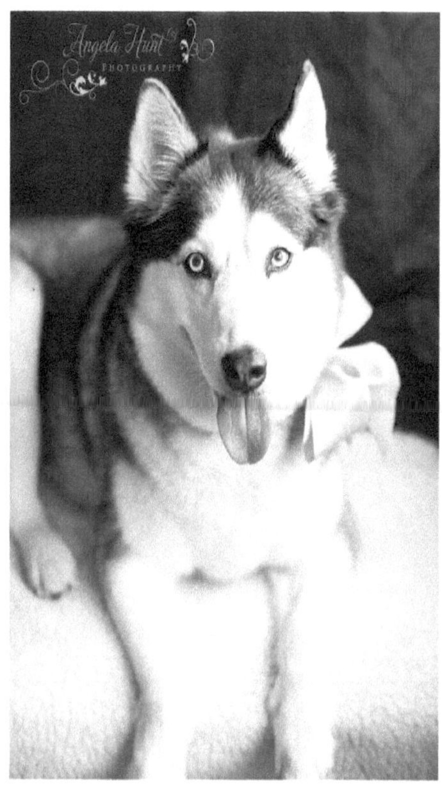

10. Do remember that your effort is for the animals. You'll have to find a place in an already-functioning system, so ease in quietly and do your best to make everyone's work easier.

And once you begin to produce good photos, you might have the opportunity to snap dogs for other rescue groups, too. The image below is Oliver, the mascot of Pit Bull Happenings, a rescue group in my area. Now Oliver is happily in his forever home, and I hope this photo will convince others that pit bulls don't deserve the bad rap they've been given.

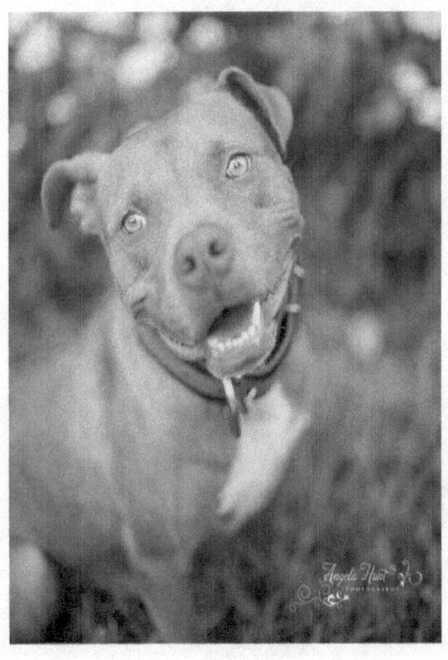

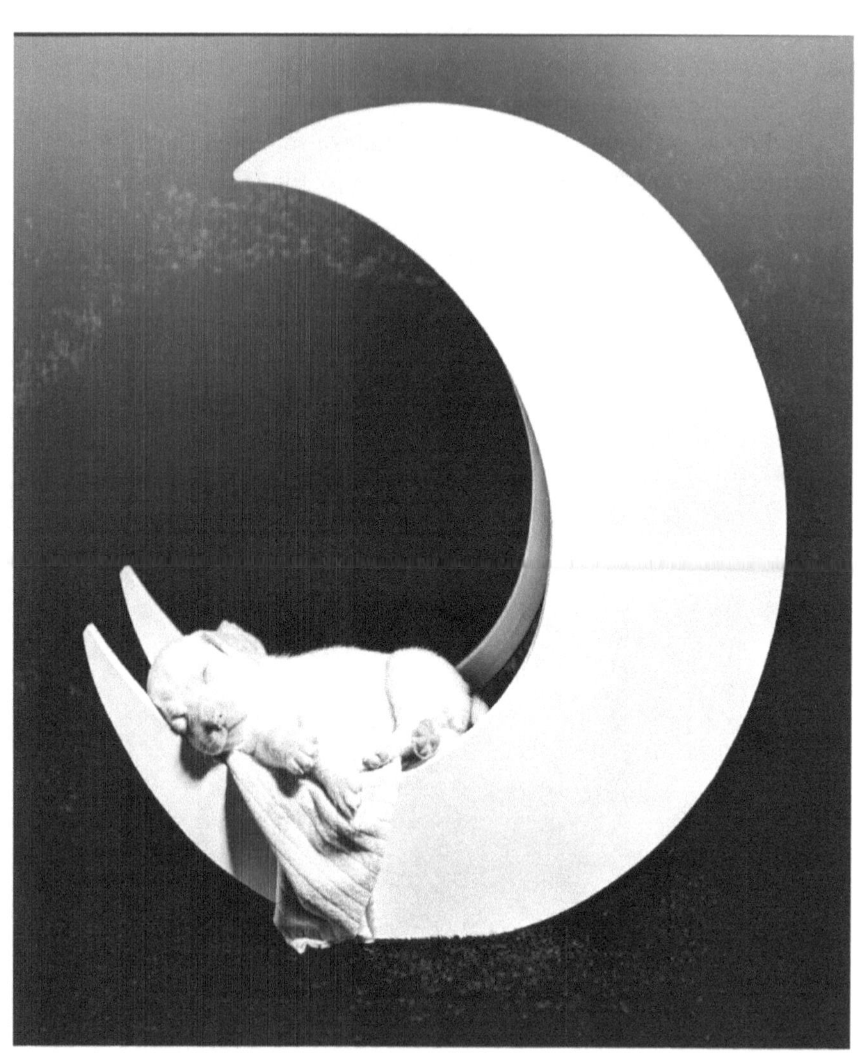

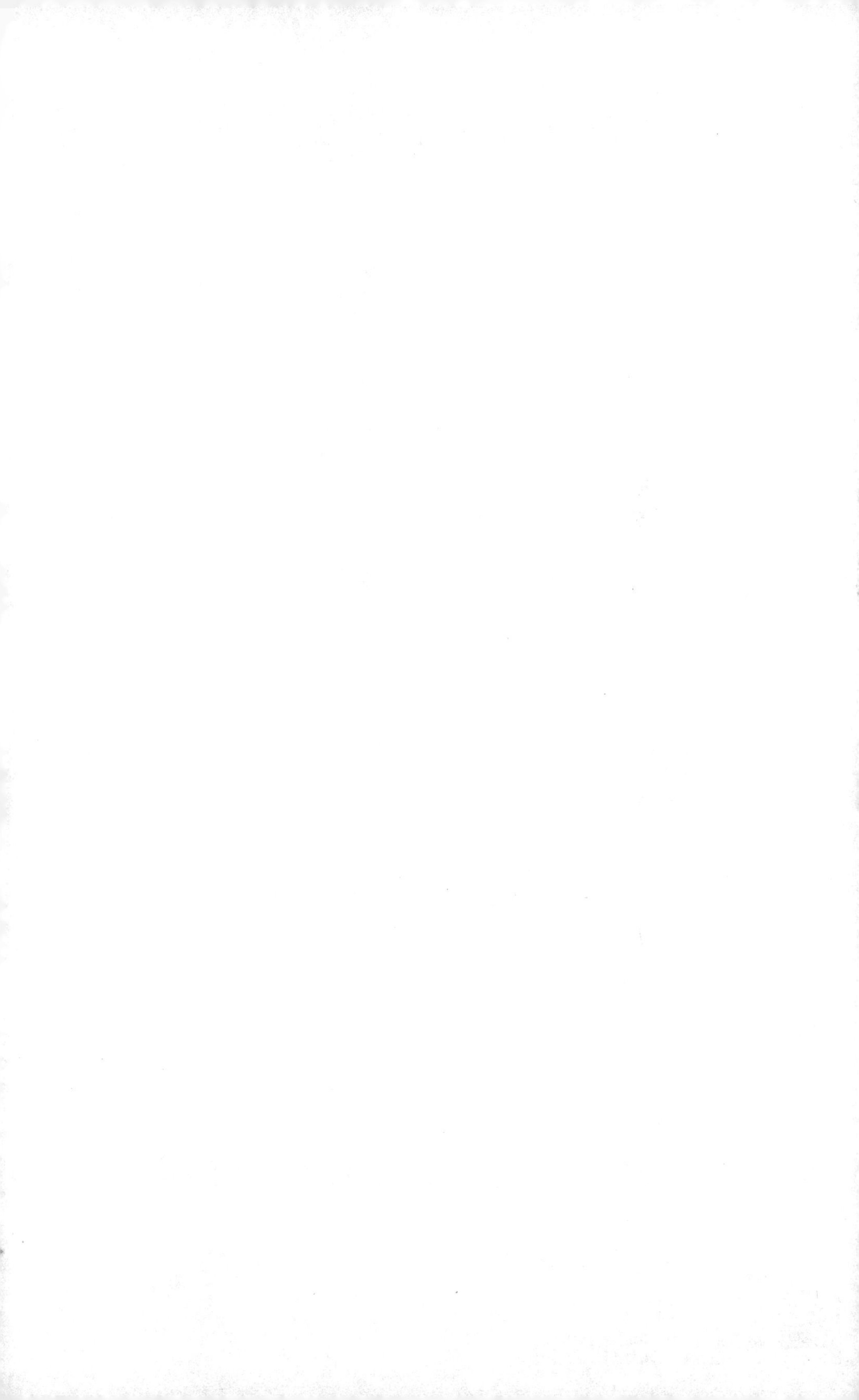